The First Time I Saw Her Face

LINDA KEATING

Illustration by Sarah Krussel

ISBN: 1497488877
ISBN-13: 978-1497488878

Acknowledgements

The completion of this book would never have been possible without the help of some very special people. I hope you all know how much I appreciate you and thank you from the bottom of my heart for your help and support.

Christina Sorenson, OD, ABCMO, thank you for helping me realize how important it was that I write this book, you were so right. The foreword you wrote is so wonderful, and thank you for taking such good care of my eyes.

Trish Hart, Friend, Editor and Author, thank you so much for the many hours you spent editing this book for me, you did a fantastic job. You had such a special way of helping me find the words I needed. You brought so much beauty to this book, I will always be grateful to you.

Sarah Krussel, Artist, Animator, Graphic Designer, and Illustrator, you came into my life at the perfect moment. You are incredibly talented, giving and kind. As I faced more challenges near the completion of the book, you stepped in and helped make it happen for me. I could never thank you enough!

Cynthia Low, PhD, you have been a wonderful friend for many years. Thank you for the beautiful foreword you wrote and for being there for me through some pretty tough times. You're the best.

Rhiannon Rubadue, Friend and Author, you helped me more than you know. You pointed me in the right direction and gave me great advice. Thank you for being such a good friend.

Oliver, I'm so happy I found you. You always have been and continue to be the best dog anyone could hope for. Thank you for your help, devotion and love, there will never be another like you.

Matthew, I would need to write another book just to thank you for everything. I'm so happy I get to share this life with you. I love and adore you. Let the adventure continue!

Table of Contents

Foreword

Doctors are privileged with an intimate knowledge of our patients, the person who lives behind the curtain. I met Linda a few years ago when she was referred to me for care by a colleague. Upon meeting Linda her vulnerability was immediately endearing. What is most striking, however, is the poised strength Linda possesses. Linda had met, endured and ultimately surmounted multiple visual challenges at a very young age. This graceful resolve remains absolutely enviable.

Linda has been an inspiration to me over the years and I am confident her story will pluck a chord for you as well. Enjoy the read!

Christina M. Sorenson, OD, ABCMO

I first met Linda in the late 1990's, as I was working with her husband. We easily became fast friends, which may have been due in part to my ability to relate to her, more so than most, because of my own vision problems. Mine are not nearly as severe as Linda's but I am very nearsighted and I know we were able to empathize with each other on that level.

As our friendship grew, I became more amazed at her fortitude and tenacity in dealing with her many struggles. I witnessed many of the problems Linda describes in her book: the failed and emergency surgeries, various surgical complications, and the loss of independence. Most people would not have fared nearly so well with the continued adversity and disappointments. However, Linda is blessed with a wonderful support system. Her husband Matthew is absolutely the most supportive, patient, and thoughtful husband one could ask for. Her family, friends, Oliver, and her faith have also sustained her. Linda is also an incredibly optimistic individual who is able to focus more on her blessings than on her losses. She is an inspiration and I am honored to be able to call her my friend.

Cynthia A. Low, Ph.D.

Chapter 1

A THOUSAND GRASSHOPPERS

There was no telling what I was thinking. I probably looked puzzled and somewhat afraid, while sitting on his lap. I'm sure he had a warm heart, and a kind and gentle touch. I was told he was Santa Claus, but to me his long white beard and bright red suit would have just appeared to be a blur of red and white splotches, I was only two-years old at the time.

I don't remember that day, but I have a photo of it. I can only imagine the confusion I felt as a baby and toddler, seeing the world through my impaired eyes. Eyes that no one else knew were only giving me some light and images that ran together. Everything I saw just looked like large and small paint splotches.

I was born in Kentucky. Our family moved to Colorado when I was about two years old. One of my favorite memories of living in that first home in Colorado was sitting on the milk box on our front porch. I would look out at the fuzzy world waiting patiently for the milkman to deliver our milk. Even though I couldn't see anything,

I must have felt really safe there. Plus, I really loved the milk and probably wanted to get the first drink from the new jar.

I was the youngest of four children. I remember being pushed on the swing by my brother and sisters. Mom and my siblings would scold me for screaming so much when I was on the swing. What no one understood was that my screams were probably from sheer terror. I had no idea where the ground began, or ended. I understand now what I must have been feeling when I was way up high in the air with everything around me looking like, well; like nothing. What is, for most kids, one of the most enjoyable experiences in life, being pushed on a swing, must have been a horrifying experience for me.

One particular day really stands out in my memory. I was in the backyard playing. Mom called me to come inside. As I approached the back patio, I came to a sudden stop at the edge of the grass and started screaming and crying. I couldn't step onto the patio because it appeared to be covered with giant grasshoppers. Mom couldn't understand why I was so scared since there were only a few of them. She tried to convince me that I had nothing to be afraid of, and that they wouldn't hurt me. She didn't realize that those few harmless grasshoppers looked to me like giant pods that appeared to blanket the entire patio! She had to pick me up and carry me inside. I can only imagine what the neighbors were thinking, when they heard my blood curdling screams.

Before I started school I was home with Mom during the day. I would "watch" television on and off throughout the day. I must have really enjoyed the sound of it, because I sure didn't see any of it. I would listen to the commercials and when Dad came home from work, I would perform all of them for him, word for word. My family had no idea that my performances were based on what I heard, not what I saw.

I had my own bedroom and remember getting extremely upset when my sisters would move anything or take something from my room. Mom would tell them to leave my things alone, that I was very particular and didn't like it when my things were rearranged or missing. I had every inch of my room; my entire home for that matter, completely memorized. They didn't realize how traumatic it was when I couldn't find something where I left it. When I would play outside with our neighborhood friends, I remember pulling back. I didn't participate as actively as the other kids. I must have somehow been aware of the times when I needed to keep a safe distance from the activities that could cause me harm. It's a miracle that I was never hurt badly. Sure, I looked both ways when I crossed the street, but only because I was told to do so. The Lord must have been watching over me because I would have never seen a car coming. My hearing senses must have been working very hard!

Speaking of senses, my sister recently shared something with me that I didn't remember. Apparently, I smelled every bite of food before putting it into my mouth. Hey, I'm positive I wanted to be sure that Mom wasn't giving me something horrible, like liver or cooked spinach! To this day, I still have a very keen sense of smell. My nose has never let me down.

My dad's job required him to travel frequently, which left Mom alone to take care of four kids. Since my eyes weren't functioning properly from the day I was born, she had no way of knowing that something was terribly wrong. She just thought that I was overly sensitive. I had mastered getting around in my little world so well, that my lack of vision wasn't obvious to my family. My Mom recalls my kindergarten teacher casually mentioning, that maybe I should get my eyes checked. She didn't tell my Mom that my nose was practically touching the screen of the Etch-A-Sketch in order to see the lines that I was drawing, while I turned those little white knobs.

3

Shortly after my kindergarten year, my Dad was transferred and we would be moving from Colorado to Nebraska. My parents decided to wait until after the move to have my eyes checked, they had no idea how severe my visual impairment was.

Since my Mom didn't drive and Dad was out of town so much, we didn't make it to the eye doctor before I started school in Nebraska. On the frightening first day of my first grade year, Mom walked me to school, took me into my classroom and explained to my teacher that I may have a little bit of trouble seeing some things, and asked if I could be seated in the front row.

After mom left and all of the students were settled in, Mrs. Johnson stood in front of my desk and introduced herself to the class. Although her image was a blur, the sound of her voice was very friendly, and her scent was so sweet that all I could do was smile, my fear had left me, and I felt happy and safe.

After Mrs. Johnson introduced herself, and made everyone feel welcome, she began to single out each student and would ask them a question. When she got to me she asked, "Linda, can you tell me what's written on the chalkboard?"

I looked up at her blurred image, and the smile fell from my face as I answered, "What chalkboard?"

That was the day my world would begin to change.

Chapter 2

LEAVES

I couldn't see Mrs. Johnson's reaction to my "what chalkboard" response, but I could feel it. I think everyone was shocked, because no one made a sound for what seemed to be a very long time; the silence was deafening. I didn't understand why, because I still didn't know what chalkboard she was talking about. Mrs. Johnson broke the uncomfortable silence by asking another student a question, which took the attention away from me. She was a true professional and a very kind person. She did what she could to minimize my embarrassment but understood that she was dealing with something very serious.

When the recess bell rang, Mrs. Johnson came to me and said, "Linda, I would like for you to come with me to the nurse's office."

She held my hand as we made our way down the hall, and I remember the concern in her voice as she gently placed me in the care of the nurse. The nurse sat me in a chair and asked me if I could see what was written on the wall, and of course I couldn't so she called my mom and told her that she needed to come and pick me up from school and take me to see an eye doctor right away.

I have no recollection of my mom picking me up, and I have no memory of the trip to the eye doctor, but I have a very clear memory of sitting in a huge chair in his office. Because of my small size, I had to sit up on my knees in order to peer through the instruments. Mom was in tears as she watched me struggle so hard for so long, to try and see something, anything. The exam seemed as though it would never end, and my mom asked the doctor to please stop so that I could rest; I was exhausted. The doctor apologized but encouraged us both to continue, until the testing was complete. He went on to explain that I was extremely nearsighted and he was having difficulty determining the right amount of correction that was needed. The exam was *finally* over, and the results were in. My prescription was a -18 and I had a *severe* astigmatism. A -18 is a big number, and seemed even bigger being attached to such a small person.

Mom was in shock, she just couldn't relate to how impaired I was, and I certainly didn't understand it. We were able to order a pair of glasses that day, but would have to wait a week or two for them to arrive, so I had to stay home from school until they came in. From that point on, things would change; my mother became much more protective of me. Mom tells me that she didn't want to let me out of her sight. She would follow me around the house, stay as close as she could to me. She wanted to do *everything* for me but she was amazed at how well I functioned and did things for myself. She made sure my siblings never let me go anywhere without them. I remember her telling all of them, "Always hold that baby's hand!"

Mom finally got the call that my glasses were ready to be picked up. Let me take you on a trip down memory lane; back to 1966 when pink, catlike, horn-rimmed glasses were in style! Those were the glasses I would wear, and they were a half-inch thick! They were the classic example of, "Coke bottle glasses."

One of my earliest and fondest memories was how my mom's hair felt. I just loved to touch her long, wavy, brown hair, and it always *smelled so good.* I would drink in the aroma every time I was close to her. Her touch was gentle, loving and kind, and she wore such vibrant colored clothing, that even though I couldn't see her clearly, it was never difficult for me to recognize her.

I knew how much I loved her, but what I didn't know, until the day I got my glasses, was what her face actually looked like. The day we walked out of the doctor's office with me donning my new, beautiful, pink, horn-rimmed eye glasses. I was thrilled beyond belief, but that thrill turned to a stunning sense of awe when I looked up at my mother's face and softly said, "Mom, you are so pretty."

That was the first time I saw her face… I can only imagine what she was feeling inside, as I watched a single tear roll down her cheek. She knelt down and gave me a big hug, clasped my hand in hers, smiled and said, "Let's take a walk, there are many pretty things for you to see."

As we walked home I saw a whole new world! I was six-years old and it was the first time that I could see buildings, cars, houses, fences, grass, flowers, streetlights, even the cracks in the sidewalk filled me with a sense of wonderment. Mom said that I was so happy, and that it was one of the most exciting and heartwarming experiences of her life, as she watched me point out all of the amazing things that I was seeing clearly for the first time, which was—*everything!* She said at one point, I stopped and looked up at the trees that were surrounding us. I asked her what all of the little green things were, and she gladly explained that they were leaves. I had heard the word leaves, but it never made sense to me. Trees had always looked like big, clumps of green, with something brown coming out the bottom. To this day, trees are one my favorite things in life.

Mom said my brother and sisters were shocked when they saw me for the first time with my glasses but much to their credit, they didn't make me feel awkward. They treated me just as they always had. They loved me and never made me feel ashamed of wearing my glasses. When I think back on how awestruck I was seeing my mom so clearly for the first time, I'm a little dumbfounded by the fact that I have no distinctive memories of seeing my siblings or my Father for the first time. I attribute that to how powerful the bond and the love are between a mother and a child.

Mom described a conversation her and my Dad had one evening before bed after he came home from traveling. She said, at first, Dad was sure the doctor had made a mistake. "There is no way her eyes could be that bad, how did we miss it, how could we not have known?!"

Mom said they felt horrible beyond words, for leaving me in such an impaired state for so long, that they held each other and cried.

The following days, weeks and months were an incredible journey for me. *Wow*, my little mind was on overload. It seemed like Christmas every day, experiencing so many new, fun things. My family says I was always a happy little girl. How could I not have been happy? I got to experience an awakening that few ever get a chance to. I was only 6 years old, but I remember thinking, how wonderful everything was!

My Mom is 81 years old now. I spoke with her about that wonderful day we walked home together. She said something she's never said before and it touched me deeply. She said, "That day felt as wonderful as the day I brought you home from the hospital, just like you were born again."

Illustrated By Sarah Krussel

Chapter 3

KIDS CAN BE MEAN

The first days back to school were wonderful in many ways. I felt like I could do anything. There was so much I was experiencing for the first time, the whole world really. It was so nice to see people's faces. All of those wonderful things were quickly diminished because, unfortunately, not only could I see their faces, but also their reaction to me and my thick glasses. With adults it was mainly looks of pity and then a smile or they would stare a bit, and look away. But the kids were a whole different story. The teasing and constant bullying began almost immediately, and it didn't stop until I was thirteen years old.

I was called names like, "coke bottle", "four eyes", "blindy", "stupid", and "retard." At school, I only heard my name spoken by my teachers, other adults, and the one or two friends that I had. I didn't have many friends throughout my school years because Dad's job transferred him about every 3 years, so I was always starting over in a new neighborhood, and a new school. That can be hard enough, but when you were the new kid *and* you wore glasses like mine, you were an immediate target for harassment. Only the truly sweet, kind girls were willing to be my friend and I will be forever grateful to them. There were so few, I still remember all of their first names: Teeka, Wendy, Stacey, and Tami. Those kind hearted girls looked past my thick glasses and took the time to actually get to know me.

At school I was subjected to many different types of abuses and bullying. Name calling and being completely ignored were bad enough, but the deepest hurt was when someone wouldn't even sit by me, as if I were a monster. When we were told to get into groups for different reasons, I would be excluded. I was never picked to be on an academic team, even though I was very smart. In gym class or on the playground, I was never picked for a sports team. I was always the last one standing there waiting with high hopes that someone would call my name. Those hopes were always dashed when the teacher would step in and force a team to take me. I lost count of how many times the kids tried to hit me in the face with different types of balls in an effort to try to break my glasses. When we had swimming class, I couldn't wear my glasses. The kids knew I couldn't see so they would call out my name. I could hear their laughter as I desperately searched for who was calling out to me.

When I was in the third grade, there were a group of kids who were bullies. They were led by a girl named Sandra. Sandra verbally abused me every day, inside or outside of the school. I was definitely afraid of her, as were other kids. I remember one day as clearly as I remember yesterday. It was lunch time and the halls were packed full of kids rushing to the cafeteria. As I made my way down the hall, Sandra came walking past me and slugged me in the stomach so hard that I fell down. After I was helped to my feet, I walked down the hall, slumped over from the pain and the horror of being assaulted, for just simply being me. I went into the bathroom, threw up and cried. I told a teacher, but nothing was done, so I just went on with my day acting as if it didn't happen.

I don't recall exactly why or where she went, but fortunately for me and the other kids that Sandra tormented; she just wasn't around anymore, she must have moved. I still find myself wondering how her life turned out, and if she ever looks back on the trauma that she so callously caused her innocent victims, and I also wonder if she feels any type of remorse. I am so happy that today, there is a greater awareness of bullying, and I am equally as sad for the kids that have taken their lives because of it. My heart and prayers go out to those families in ways you can only imagine, having lived through so many horrible moments of bullying.

When I finished fifth grade, we left Nebraska and moved back to Colorado for a few years. There were a few kids who decided to get to know me; they were a little group of kids who were considered to be, "misfits". We all had one thing or another that was different, and that marked us as easy targets for the school bullies. One of the little girls had some kind of nerve problem and had no control over her mouth. It would open and close and go from a frown to a smile repeatedly all day long. The other kids and the teachers didn't understand this so they gave her a hard time. I remember a teacher being really mean to her while asking her what she was smiling at. I explained to the teacher that she couldn't help it—it's not just kids that are mean!

Even though it was so tough for me at school, I had fun at home with my family. My brother and sisters and I were always up to something, especially when Mom and Dad weren't home. We had fun playing silly games; my sisters would pick on each other and then take it out on my brother by dressing him up in crazy outfits. And, of course, there was the night all three of them were holding onto me, teaching me to ski down our long coffee table which was propped up against the back of the couch!

Three years after moving back to Colorado, we were on the move again. That time we moved to Salt Lake City, Utah. Those would prove to be some of my most difficult school years. Once again, I was the new kid. It was my first day of sixth grade. At that time, the majority of people living in Salt Lake City were members of The Church of Jesus Christ of Latter Day Saints, more commonly known as Mormons. I didn't know anything about Mormons. I don't believe my parents did either because it was not discussed prior to us moving there. It may have helped to know what a Mormon was, because the first words spoken to me by a few of the kids when I walked into school were, "Are you a Mormon?"

Not, "Hello, where are you from?" Or, "What is your name?"

By that time I had a defense mechanism in place where I would use silly humor to ward off difficult questions. I giggled and said, "No, I'm not a Mormon, I'm a girl!" Well, that didn't go over well so needless to say, I had fewer friends than ever. Not only was I not a Mormon, which meant automatic exclusion, but I still had my beautiful, pink, thick, horn-rimmed glasses. I just couldn't figure out why no one liked them when I was so in love with them. They were the best present I had ever received. When you receive a precious gift such as your sight, it's hard to despise the package it's wrapped in, no matter how difficult it makes your life. I came home from school on many days, and cried from being treated so badly.

I remember one time when I was in sixth grade, my Mom came to school, and the teacher allowed her to speak to my class. Mom told all of my classmates about the day I got my glasses and why I needed them. She explained to them that I was a nice, smart little girl who didn't deserve to be treated the way they were treating me. She asked them to give me a chance, to take time to get to know me and try to see past my glasses. What came from that was a friendship that meant everything to me for the rest of the time I lived there. A girl named Stacey came and sat by me and asked me to have lunch with her. I have since lost contact with her, but I would love to see her again and thank her.

From sixth to ninth grade, I was teased and bullied relentlessly. At that age, of course, I liked boys and wanted them to like me back. Not even one boy gave me any attention. Some would be cordial to me during forced school events, but never at any other time. Most boys ignored me; some would tease and bully me repeatedly. I never let it stop me from trying to participate because I was determined to have fun, and be a part of the same activities that all of the other kids enjoyed.

One of my biggest blows was when I participated in a teen Mormon Church group. It was on Wednesday nights; it was called, "Mutual." We sat in a circle in the beginning. The group leader, an adult, asked me to say the first prayer for the night. I started out my little prayer, "Dear Lord," and the snickering and giggling began, it is bad enough when other kids laugh at you, but it paled in comparison to how small I felt having an adult join in, and that's exactly what the leader of that group did.

Apparently I didn't start the prayer in a way they were accustomed to. I had gotten used to being teased and made fun of for my glasses, but that was the first time in my life I was teased about the way I prayed! Often when I was young, I would pray we wouldn't have to move again. When we lived in Salt Lake City, I prayed every day that we would.

When I turned 13, I was in the 9th grade and still living in Salt Lake City. I begged my parents to let me get contact lenses. The glasses I was wearing at that time had a more modern frame, but I wanted so badly, not to have to wear them at all. My parents finally agreed and convinced the doctor that I was very responsible, and would take care of them.

I was certain that my life would change when I got contacts, but boy was I wrong. Everyone was in such a habit of treating me so poorly that nothing changed and the bullying continued.

I didn't have to suffer for much longer because right after I got my contact lenses, my Dad was being transferred again. I smiled at the thought of my coke bottle glasses being nothing but a cruel memory. I cut off my long, bushy, out of control hair, and grew boobs! I was heading towards a new adventure, a brand new life, with a whole new look, and no one would know that little girl who had so much working against her. That Linda was soon to be set free and the real Linda that had spent so many years trapped in a twisted maze of cruel circumstances, was ready to really start living! One of my greatest hopes and wishes would finally come true; I would live in a world where everyone would just simply call me, "Linda..." —Phoenix, Arizona, here I come!

I'm so glad, that as an adult, I can look back on my past as being an unfortunate childhood experience. I'm not bitter towards anyone, and I'm certainly not bitter towards Mormons. In fact, some of my closest friends are of the Mormon faith, and I absolutely love Salt Lake City. I still have family there and it's one of my favorite places to visit.

Sometimes I wonder how I got through all of those difficult years of the teasing and the bullying. It was my family that kept me strong; it was because of their love and support that I retained all of my self-worth. They always made me feel like I was a special person. They never let me doubt myself, or wonder whether or not I was good enough.

I never stopped telling myself, that I knew I was a good person that could be strong, happy and positive no matter what life would throw at me. Of course, there were many times that I experienced deep sadness, but I was determined to never allow anyone to take my happiness away from me. Living amongst all of those who tried to beat me down; I would often remind myself, that I was worthy, and I would not let the cruel people win; break my spirit, or determine my future.

Chapter 4

THE NEW ME

*P*hoenix was awesome! Warmth, sunshine, high school, and a brand new me…..WOW!

Life had definitely changed. I started at my new school in February. I was the new kid again, but that was okay, because I felt new. I appreciated my glasses because of the sight they gave me, but the new contacts were fantastic. I was able to see a little better with them, but even with my corrective glasses and my contact lenses, my doctors were not able to get my vision to 20/20. The best I ever achieved was 20/40, but that was enough for me. Since the contacts sat directly on the eye, they could improve the vision a bit and help with the astigmatism.

It felt great to walk into a room and be treated like a normal person. No one looked away, no one laughed at me, other students asked me what my name was, and they actually talked to me! In Utah, I was in junior high as a 9th grader. It was fine with me being at the bottom, as a freshman, in Phoenix. I was ecstatic to just be in high school!

My high school years were not much different than most kids. I had many, new, fun, exciting experiences. I wasn't hugely popular, but hey, I wasn't an outcast. I loved school. I studied hard and got very good grades. I wasn't into sports but I loved drama, and I took dance, speech and business courses. I became part of a program called, Cooperative Office Education which prepared me for work in an office environment. I had a couple of part-time jobs during my senior year, but my first full-time job right before I graduated, and for a few years after, was a Mortgage Loan Processor. I was only seventeen years old, and had my own office on the eighteenth floor of a fancy, high-rise building in downtown Phoenix.

I dated a few guys, but had a long standing relationship with a guy named, Mark. After graduation, we broke up and he went into the Army. I was having a great time dating, spending time with friends, working full-time, attending community college, and taking dance classes. I became part of a dance company. After about a year our dance company was offered the opportunity to perform in Las Vegas, as background dancers in the shows. That was all very excit-ing, but there was one complication, Mark and I had gotten back together, and he asked me to marry him. I was only twenty years old, and instead of following my dream of dancing, I got married. At that age, you think that you are always going to have the chance to pursue those dreams again.

Shortly after Mark and I got married, he got transferred to Germany. We lived there for a total of 6 years with only a 1 year break in between, at a post in the USA. Although I didn't continue my college education, I have to say that being able to live in Europe for six years was an outstanding education! It was a wonderful experience that I would never trade. I traveled extensively to dif-ferent countries and experienced different cultures. I learned to snow ski in Switzerland, (which was much better than the coffee table), I stood at the top of the Eiffel Tower in Paris, parasailed in

Spain, rode a gondola in Venice, and saw the beautiful country of Yugoslavia before it was destroyed by war. That was a great journey that I thoroughly enjoyed throughout my twenties.

I had a wonderful time in Europe, but unfortunately, my marriage was not a strong, happy one. I believe it only lasted as long as it did because of the unique life we were living overseas. We came home to the USA and our work took us to Tucson, Arizona and then San Diego, California for a short time. I reminded myself that I would not allow anyone to take my happiness away from me, so shortly after moving to San Diego, Mark and I decided to get a divorce. As the divorce was being finalized, I moved back to Phoenix, where I still had a lot of friends. I stayed with my parents while I looked for work.

It wasn't long before I was hired as a marketing assistant for a company that set jewels into plaques, pins, and pendants for achievement awards. I was enjoying the first few days at my job, and looked for an apartment to rent that was closer to work. My two bosses called me in one afternoon to let me know I was doing a great job. During that conversation, I mentioned to them that I hadn't had a chance to tell my brother about my new job. I told them that he would be very happy for me because in the early days of his career, he was in this same type of business. They looked quite surprised and asked me his name. When I told them they were speechless. As it turned out, they both knew my brother very well; they had worked with him many years earlier and he basically taught them the business. Talk about a small world!

The next morning, I arrived at work happy and excited for the future. I poured a cup of coffee and shortly after sitting down at my desk, my bosses called me into their office again; I was thinking, *wow these guys must really think I'm a great employee but* a few minutes into the conversation, they fired me.

They were apologetic, but they said they just couldn't take the risk that I might "leak" sensitive business information to my brother. I was sad, angry and shocked! I explained to them that my brother hadn't been in that end of the business for a long time, and that he had his own jewelry company. What in the world could I ever tell him, and more importantly, why would I? I was so insulted that they questioned my integrity and my brothers'; after all he had done for them.

My 30 minute drive home was like a bad, slow motion dream. I couldn't believe what happened. I walked into my parent's house, it was late morning. My Dad made a joke; he said, "Why are you home so early, did you get fired?" I burst into tears and said *"yes!"* Poor Dad, he ran to me, hugged me, and apologized for his joke. I called and let my brother know what happened and needless to say he was pretty angry, he couldn't believe it. He said he was going to call those guys and let them have it. I'm sure they felt like gum on the bottom of a shoe by the time he was finished with them.

Getting through a divorce and having such an awful thing happen with my new job was so hard that I threw myself a pity party that lasted a day or two, but I reminded myself what I had learned at a young age, that I would not allow the "bullies" to win or determine my future! I dove into the classified ads a few days later and found an advertisement for a job that sounded amazing. I called them on Monday, and was asked to come in for an interview.

The position was for the Office Manager and Employee Recruiter at a waterpark. That was definitely a job that was a better fit for my personality, and I was very excited at the thoughts of landing it. The weather on the day of my interview was very stormy. It was raining and extremely windy. I walked into the waterpark and saw two guys off in the distance, digging a deep hole. They waved at me, so I asked them where the office was located. They pointed me in the right direction, and off I went. By the time I got inside, my nice outfit and my hair had been blown to bits. I'm sure I looked like a big mess! In spite of my appearance, my interview went so well, that I was offered the job the next day.

The pay was better than my previous job, it was closer to where I wanted to live, and the potential future success of the waterpark made that opportunity, fantastic! I knew that job was going to be great in many ways, but I had no idea that it would be a life altering event that was obviously meant to be, because waiting for me there, digging a hole, and giving me directions; was the love of my life…

Chapter 5

MATTHEW

I began my new job at Waterworld, and besides the account-ing, which was very challenging for me visually, and the brutally long hours, I really enjoyed it. The waterpark was closed for the season when I started. Other than myself and a couple of part-time high school girls that worked for me, there were about ten men working there. They were nice guys and we all had good working relationships. There was one guy that stood out from all of the rest, his name was, Matthew.

Matthew was one of those people that everyone liked, including me. He was approachable and easy to talk to. I knew the minute I met him, that he was smart, kind, funny and someone who I could trust completely. We had opportunities throughout each day to talk to one another and it was obvious that he enjoyed our conversations as much as I did. Although I liked Matthew, I had no interest in a romantic relationship; my divorce was almost final, and I wanted to focus on my work and just be single for a while. I knew I would like to date and even get married again someday, but I made a promise to myself that I would never settle again. I was determined not to repeat the cycle of being with a man that I was not truly happy with. I knew what I wanted in a partner and I would know when I found him, no matter how long it took.

I needed some shelves put up in my office and Matthew came in to hang them. We decided that the shelves would look better if they were stained so he offered to come back the next day.

I went home that night and couldn't wait for a new day to begin just so I could spend more time with Matthew, but at the same time a nagging inner voice of reason would interrupt my dreamy thoughts; *stop it with the crush on Matthew, you're going to take your time, remember? And besides, he is too sweet, too handsome and six-years younger than you. Your divorce isn't even final—and just because he enjoys talking to you; it doesn't mean that he wants to be in a relationship with you!*

I went back to work the next day and Matthew came into my office and began to stain the shelves. We talked about a variety of things; jumping from one subject to another. After a while, we couldn't say anything to each other without laughing, I mean we were laughing hysterically. People were walking by my office giving us the strangest looks. I had no windows in my office and very little ventilation. We came to realize we were getting completely high off of the fumes from the stain! That stuff takes a while to wear off too, wow, what a headache I had.

I was developing a major crush on Matthew, and was fighting it hard. I could tell he enjoyed talking with me, but I really didn't think that a sweet, handsome guy, who was six years younger than I was, would be interested in me like I was him. Not to mention, that my divorce wasn't even out of the oven yet! So I tried hard to convince myself that I was only interested in having him as a good friend. It was Valentine's Day and I had been at my job for a little over two weeks. Matthew and

I pulled into work at about the same time. I walked up to him as he stood at the entrance and I asked him, "What are you doing"?

He said, "Waiting for you."

The way his voice sounded when he said that to me, made me feel like I was going to melt into my shoes. I was perplexed by how strong my feelings were for a man that I had only known for two weeks, and I knew that I had to get control of myself.

A few days later a group of us at work planned to go out to lunch. Everyone backed out for one reason or another, so it ended up being just Matthew and I. We called our orders in ahead of time and we ordered the exact same thing. I felt so comfortable with him and I could tell he was a very positive thinker, just like me. I knew I could tell him anything, so as we were eating our lunch, I confided in him and told him that I was in the process of getting a divorce. As he listened to my story about my failed marriage, his responses were mature, kind and thoughtful. I could tell that he was a very special person. It was hard to believe that he was only twenty three years old. He told me that he was born and raised in a small town in Iowa. After going to college for one year, he decided to join the Navy, because he wanted to see the world. He had just gotten out of the Navy a few months earlier and decided to move to Arizona. His best friend, Steve, was living there so he thought it would be a great place to begin the next part of his life. Steve was working at the waterpark, so Matthew started working there while he figured out which career path he was going to follow.

We talked about all of the things that we liked to do when we weren't working. We both liked to take long walks and go hiking so we decided to take a hiking trip on our next day off. My ex-husband didn't enjoy doing many things with me, and he definitely wouldn't take a walk or go hiking. I couldn't believe that I met such a nice guy who was willing to do those things with me and I was happy to know that Matthew and I were going to be great friends.

I drove to his apartment early in the morning and we took his car to the hiking spot. From the minute we got in the car, and throughout the entire hike, there was never a lull in the conversation. We talked about everything and got to know each other. It was unbelievable to us how much we had in common; everything from our favorite foods, cars, music, and spiritual beliefs. We laughed at how uncanny it all was. We both loved to dance so we made plans to go dancing the following weekend. I was really starting to like him, and it didn't help that he was so handsome and sexy. He was hiking in front of me, and it got very hot outside so he took off the sweat pants that he had on over his tight hiking shorts. Mercy—*what a view!* He had a great body. After we got back to his place we went inside to get something to drink and cool off. We sat across the room from each other and talked for a while longer and the mutual attraction and feelings of desire became very intense, so I decided I had better get out of there quick.

As I drove home, I wrestled with feelings that I had never felt before, but I kept holding on to the thought that it was only going to be a friendship, and I knew I had better settle down. I couldn't help but smile and be happy because I was going to see him the next day at work.

The week at work, that lead up to our night of dancing was brutal. I was so excited but also worried that he might cancel. I could tell by the way he looked and smiled at me, that he was excited too.

I drove to his house to pick him up. I got out of my car and nervously walked up to his apartment and rang the bell. A few seconds later he opened the door, and he wasn't wearing a shirt, I could see it lying on the ironing board behind him. A lump formed in my throat as I watched him iron his shirt, he was so hot that I felt like running out of there, and I'm still not sure how I maintained my composure.

We went country western dancing, and it was like we had been lifelong dance partners, we didn't miss a beat. After dancing to several songs we decided to take a break and have a drink. He held my hand as we listened to the music and talked. We both realized that our relationship was going to be much more than just a casual friendship when Matthew looked at me and said, "I cannot believe how strongly I feel about you; only knowing you for such a short time."

Once I cleared my throat, I squeaked out my confession of feeling the same way about him.

On the drive home, we laughed as we sang to the radio at the top of our lungs. We decided we were going to take a drive to Sedona the next day, which is a beautiful, red rock area, North of Phoenix.

When we got back to his place, we stood outside for quite a while just talking and looking up at the stars, and then… he kissed me, again and again, and again. I had never, ever been kissed like that. Yes they were extremely passionate kisses, but above and beyond that, they were the most loving, emotionally powerful kisses that I had ever experienced. We went inside and well….I didn't leave until the next morning. I could not feel any shame for spending the night with him, because it was one of the most beautiful nights of my life.

Even though I was an adult woman, my parents weren't thrilled that I had spent the night with Matthew, my Dad was pretty mad at me. I called and told them that I wouldn't be home, but they were still angry and worried. I apologized for worrying them, but explained to them that Matthew was a very special man, and they would understand when they met him.

Matthew came to the house to pick me up for our trip to Sedona. He walked up to our front door with his head held high, looked my Dad in the eye, shook his hand and introduced himself. When I introduced him to my Mom, he smiled and looked at her with those big green eyes and dimples in his cheeks, and gave her a hug. She was smitten with him. They both forgot all about being angry, they adored him. Like I said before, there was no way you wouldn't like Matthew the minute you met him.

My Dad always said, "I knew Matthew was a good man when he had the nerve to walk up and shake my hand the day after he kept my daughter out all night!"

Matthew and I spent the entire day in Sedona and we had a wonderful time. As he was driving us back to Phoenix, I was looking out the window and I pointed out something that I thought was beautiful. He looked over at me and said, "I think we are going to see a lot of beautiful things together."

We were only together for two weeks when he looked at me one evening and told me that he loved me by pointing to himself, then his heart and then to me. I put my arms around him and told him that I loved him too. We were both very aware of how soon it was to be feeling the way we did, but neither of us doubted or had reservations about how we felt.

Even though I wore my contacts most of the time, I occasionally wore my glasses to take a break from the contacts. I remember the first time I let Matthew see me in my thick glasses. Although I was a little nervous for him to see them for the first time, I knew in my heart that he would never make me feel bad about them. He didn't mind them at all and he told me I was beautiful no matter what.

I asked Matthew if it would be ok with him if we didn't tell our co-workers right away that we were dating. I was so new at the job, I was in management, and I worried about what they would think about a recently divorced woman, getting so serious with a younger guy that she just met. He agreed, so we proceeded to try and keep our romance a secret. Rather than eat his lunch outside in the beautiful weather, Matthew would sit in the lobby just outside of my office, eat his lunch, and watch me. One day I was looking out the window at him, watching him work with no shirt on, and got caught by the girls in the office.

It was obvious that we couldn't keep our secret much longer, the day we accidently came face to face in a very small office supply room and as we passed by each other, our arms touched which caused our hearts to race and our faces to flush. We had a difficult time being close to one another without hugging and kissing—it was electric!

The guys that Matthew worked closely with were very suspicious of his unusual behavior. They kept prodding him for a confession, by telling him that he was acting like he was in love and they wanted to know with whom? He tried his hardest to avoid giving them a straight answer but because of his honest nature, he finally broke down and told them what they had already figured out; that he and I were dating. His confession came late in the day so he didn't have a chance to let me know that our secret was no longer a secret.

When I walked into work the next day, the guys were sitting at a table right outside of my office, where we held our morning meetings, and they were giggling like a bunch of school girls. When I walked into my office I discovered a note sitting on my desk that read:

We want coffee and donuts every morning, or we will tell.

My heart sank, but I quickly recovered when I looked up at them and they all burst out laughing.

It was a major relief that our secret was finally out, no more pretending, and the fact that everyone was so happy for us made it even easier. They said it was obvious that Matthew and I were meant for each other, and they could tell how real our love for one another was. Six months later, in August, Matthew asked me to marry him and we moved in together. We got married four months later on New Year's Eve, December 31, 1990.

As you read further you will see, like many people, we have been tested. Not our marriage, it has always been rock solid, but our strength to weather some pretty difficult storms. Rather than break us down, we maintained our positive attitudes and held on tight to one another.

I know without a doubt, I was meant to find Matthew. His love and support of me through good and bad times has never wavered. He isn't just a wonderful man and husband; he is the finest person I have ever known. As it turns out, we did become good friends; best friends.

Chapter 6

LIFE THROWS YOU CURVES

*A*fter we had been married for about a year, Matthew started his career working for the federal government. Just as I had hoped, my career moved in the direction of event planning. I was working for a large company planning a variety of large and small events and loving it.

In 1992, Matthew and I had been married for two years when I began to notice a decline in my vision, so I decided to go to an eye surgeon to see if I was a candidate for a new corrective eye surgery called, Radial Keratotomy. As soon as I got into the exam room and told them what my prescription was, they knew immediately that I wasn't a good candidate for the surgery. To be a candidate, the maximum correction for someone who was nearsighted was a -8. I was a -18 and had severe astigmatism.

I was thankful that my contacts and glasses helped me to see as well as I did, but working and driving were becoming a real challenge, so I was disappointed to find out that I wasn't a candidate

for the newest corrective surgery. The doctors saw the disappointment in my face that day and reassured me that the technology
was improving all of the time, and they would keep my case at the
front of their discussions, and would let me know if they could help
me in the future.

A few months later, the eye surgeon called and said they had a
surgery that might work for me but the surgery would have to be
performed at a clinic in Houston, Texas. A normal eye is shaped
perfectly round but I was so nearsighted, my eyes were shaped like
footballs. They were going to work on one eye at a time. They were
going to remove my cornea, freeze it, place it on a lathe, cut and
reshape it and then put it back in my eye. The end result would
hopefully be a perfectly shaped cornea that gave me close to perfect vision.

I was extremely nervous about the surgery. In addition, the surgery
wasn't covered by insurance, and there was no way that Matthew
and I could afford it. My Mom and Dad were so supportive; they
offered to pay for it. Matthew and my parents were so encouraging
and helped ease my fears. My Dad said to me, "You could have fifty
to sixty more years to live, don't you want to see the very best you
can for those years?"

Of course, my answer was, "Yes!"

Matthew couldn't get enough time off work, so my Dad was going
to travel with me to Houston. We were all very excited and anxious
to get on with it.

My doctors in Arizona were going to handle all of my pre-operative
work, but as my surgeon examined me, he saw something that deeply concerned him. He excused himself from the room, and moments later he reappeared with two other surgeons. They took turns

examining me, and were totally shocked at what they found. The lenses in both of my eyes were subluxed (dislocated). The ligaments that held the lenses in place were so weak, they were breaking. This was one of the reasons I had such a hard time focusing and was never able to achieve 20/20 vision with contacts or glasses. None of us will ever know how I could have been thirty two years old, with ongoing eye care from age-six, and no other eye doctor had *ever* told me or my parents about my lens problem. The surgeons didn't know what to think, it was something they had never seen in a normal, healthy person. Their best guess was that I was born with the problem, and the lenses would continue to go further out of place as time went on.

Because of the discovery, my doctors felt that the health of my eye was too important to risk and therefore, they could not go through with the corneal surgery in Houston. All of my hopes were dashed when the mood in the room went from excited optimism to extreme disappointment. I went home, called my parents with the news and waited for Matthew to come home so I could tell him the bad news. We had such high hopes, and to say that it was emotionally difficult to accept the sad reality of the latest diagnosis, is an extreme understatement. In spite of my disappointment, I was determined not to let it keep me down; Matthew and my parents felt bad enough, so I had to prove to them that I was okay, and would live every day to the fullest with the hopes of lessening their pain and strengthening my courage to live as normal of a life as possible. I had so much to be grateful for.

Matthew and I were loving life, working hard and saving to buy a house. Several months later, my eye surgeon called to inform me of a new and very successful surgery that had just been introduced, and he thought I would be a great candidate. The surgery was called Automated Lamellar Keratoplasty (ALK). It was an outpatient surgery, it was much less invasive than the other one, and it could be done locally in Arizona, by my own surgeon. They wouldn't have to remove my cornea; it would remain in my eye while they shaved off layers to reshape it.

Two weeks following the phone call from my doctor, they operated on my right eye with great success and my eye healed so quickly that within a few weeks I could see 20/40 out of that eye—*without contacts or glasses!* They operated on my left eye a month later with marginal success.

After both eyes were healed, they did an additional Radial Keratotomy surgery on the left eye to improve it a bit. I also achieved 20/40 vision in the left eye. They were still not able to get me to 20/20 with correction because of my dislocated lenses, but that was fine with me. I didn't wear glasses or contacts for almost a year and—*it was incredible!* After that I started working on computers and needed to wear some low power glasses most of the time. For the first time in my life, I could wear cute, fashionable glasses. The frames were beautiful and the lenses weren't thick. I was so thankful for my "new" eyes. Matthew, my parents and my entire family were so happy for me because they knew all I had gone through to get to that point. The outpouring of love and support from all of them was so heartwarming.

We bought our first house a year later. Both of our jobs were going great, I could see and life was good. Everything was going along just fine and then one night I got very ill after dinner at my parent's home. I had terrible pain in my abdomen and vomited all night long. I thought I had caught the stomach flu. I felt as good as new in about two days, but what was to follow was a nightmare. At the same time, once every month, I became sick again. The pain and vomiting would worsen each time it happened. After seeing seven doctors, and suffering with that mysterious problem for two years, I was finally diagnosed with, endometriosis. When I was thirty four, I had a complete hysterectomy and an appendectomy on the same day. Because of the repeated trauma every month, I had developed so much scar tissue in my abdomen it had attached my bowel to the lining of my stomach, and encased my appendix. After my surgery, guess what happened the next month? *Nothing!* I was never sick like that again.

Matthew and I had decided early in our marriage that we didn't want to have children, so the hysterectomy was not a difficult decision for us. The mysterious illness required me to go through so much testing that I had to stop taking birth control pills and since we didn't want a surprise pregnancy, we both agreed that it would be best for him to have a vasectomy. As he was recovering, on the couch with a bag of frozen peas on his groin, we were told that I needed to have a hysterectomy. I looked at him sheepishly, smiled and said, "Oops, I guess you didn't have to do that after all?" We got a good laugh out of that!

Matthew was such a great support through all of it. I had missed a lot of work from being sick, and towards the end of the illness, I had to stop working completely and focus on finding out how to get well. He worked a lot of overtime so that we could pay our bills. That was a big test on a young marriage, but we got through it together with hope and laughter and it made our marriage even stronger.

As time passed, Matthew was keenly aware that if he was going to get promoted in his profession, we would probably have to move someday. That opportunity came for him in 1998, so we were headed to Seattle, Washington. We were very sad to leave my parents and our friends and Arizona, but at the same time, it was exciting. Professionally it was the best thing for Matthew. The promotions happened quickly for him once he arrived in Seattle. He was finally able to work in an area that he really enjoyed and where all of his talents would be utilized.

I found a great job as the event planner for a company that manufactured kitchen gadgets and accessories. After a few years I decided to make a change and landed a job as the event planner for a city parks and recreation department. That job really suited my personality and was a perfect fit for me. We were never in love with the gloomy, gray weather in Washington and we thought about leaving a few times, but we toughed it out because we were both enjoying our jobs, and we were comfortable financially. We traveled extensively and spent time with great friends.

We were getting ready to fly to Utah to attend our niece's wedding, which was scheduled for September 13, 2001. On September 10th, we received a call from Matthew's step mom in Iowa informing us that his Dad, Robert, had been killed that morning while mowing the bank of a ditch. He was driving a tractor, pulling a brush hog (a flat mower deck) behind him. The brush hog weighs several hundred pounds. He must have hit some loose soil or was at too steep of an angle, because the tractor tipped over. Robert was thrown from the tractor into the ditch. The brush hog landed on his chest pinning him to the ground. He had his cell phone in the front pocket of his overalls and was able to call 911. Considering he was out in the country, the response time of the paramedics was quick, they reached him in less than ten minutes, but unfortunately Robert suffocated from the weight of the brush hog and died before they got to him.

That evening we rearranged our flights. Matthew would fly to Iowa for his Dad's funeral, and I would fly to Utah for the wedding. The next day, we woke up to the horrible tragedy of September 11th. Needless to say, neither of us was going to be able to fly anywhere! We had to act quickly, so we got new tires put on the car and we took off. We drove to Utah so that I could attend the wedding. Our emotions were all over the place. We were so happy for our niece with her upcoming wedding, mourning the loss of Matthew's father and wondering what was happening to our world. Matthew dropped me off with my family in Utah, and drove away to Iowa by himself. That was a very hard goodbye.

The wedding was wonderful, my niece was so happy, and I felt great being with my family. After several days, I was able to book a flight to Iowa on a small airline. I was somewhat nervous about flying after 9/11 but I needed to get to Iowa to pay my respects to the family and help Matthew drive back to Washington.

We had been through a tough time, but after things calmed down, we decided to make a fresh change and sell the condo that we purchased five years earlier when we moved to Washington. We bought a new house that we visited everyday as it was being built. Moving day was quickly approaching. We had our entire home packed. We had two days before the moving truck would arrive and all of our utilities were scheduled to be shut off. And then the call came from our realtor. The man who had purchased our condo changed his mind and backed out of the purchase! The builder of our new home couldn't hold the house for us, so we lost our new home. Needless to say, we were beyond disappointed and it wasn't fun unpacking everything that had just been packed.

We swore we would *never* move again, we would just stay in the condo—*forever!* But, never say, "Never." We tried to sell the condo again about six months later because we came across a small, cottage style house on a quarter acre that we fell in love with. We sold our condo in a few days and put an offer on the house. The house was old but had been remodeled, almost throughout. It was very small and not energy efficient so right after moving in, we had a design drawn up with plans to make it a bit larger and most importantly, warmer.

Well, as life often will, it threw us another curve. One month after moving into our house, I was laid off from my job at the park district so the remodeling plan came to a screeching halt.

While I looked for a permanent job, I decided to work for a temporary agency. I was having a great time working for a variety of companies, plus the flexibility was fantastic.

Matthew and I both loved dogs and had talked often about owning one. The house and the size of our property were perfect for having a dog. Since my work schedule was so flexible, I figured I would have time to train it and help it adjust to our home, so we decided it was the perfect time to become doggy parents.

We had no idea what a special addition we were about to make to our family.

Chapter 7

Oliver, Gorilla Warfare

We had known for years that the type of dog that we would adopt would be a Standard Poodle. I was highly allergic to cats and all dog breeds, except poodles. We had seen many Standard Poodles over the years and studied the breed. We knew this would be the best dog for us.

I called a local breeder to inquire about buying a puppy. We talked on the phone for about thirty minutes. I could tell she was very particular about who could purchase her pups, there was no guarantee that we would get one until she met both Matthew and I and was completely satisfied that we would provide a good life and lots of love for the puppy. She told me she had a three month old male that she really wanted to keep for herself because there was something very special about him, but she knew she couldn't keep him since she already had several of her own.

She must have had a good feeling about me during our phone conversation because she invited us to come meet her and her "extra special pup". We didn't take the idea of pet ownership lightly because we knew that life would change for us. On the beautiful, two hour drive to the breeder's home, Matthew and I confessed to one another that we were feeling both excited and nervous. We had always been a team, and we knew that owning a dog would only enrich our lives, even if it did add a new layer of responsibility and inconvenience.

We arrived at the picturesque home of the breeder, which was surrounded by acres of beautiful hillsides and giant pine trees; it looked like a picture that you would see on a postcard. The breeder invited us into her home where she and her husband interviewed us for almost two hours before we were allowed to meet the puppy. They were wonderful, caring people who had been breeding Standard Poodles for nearly forty years. It was clear to see that they were professionals and it was obvious that they loved their dogs. They finally took us into a cozy room near the kennels and then… they brought him in.

He was a darling, black ball of fur with dark brown eyes; he looked like a baby gorilla and he weighed approximately twenty-five pounds. He checked me out briefly, but quickly made his way over to Matthew. His handler was a man, so he seemed more comfortable with men. He really liked Matthew, but who could blame him—everyone liked Matthew. Matthew petted and played with him and they quickly became buddies. He eventually made his way over to me where I sat patiently while he approached me. I let him sniff around to get to know me before I played with him. When I scooped him up, and petted his soft warm belly, he felt so comfortable in my arms that he went limp and relaxed completely. When he looked up at me with those sweet brown eyes, I knew that he was mine; I knew he was going home with us and I knew that I was in love.

It was obvious to the breeder that her pup was in good hands with Matthew and I and she was thrilled that she had found the perfect owners who were worthy of her special boy. She was also happy to know we had already picked out a name for him; we would call him "Oliver."

We were both tired so we took turns driving home. I drove first and Matthew held Oliver in his lap. Matthew got behind the wheel at the half-way mark; it was my turn to hold Oliver and enjoy his warm little body sitting on my lap, he was so sweet!

As we drove down the highway, Oliver would tremble; he would be still for a few moments and then start trembling again. I told Matthew that he was probably scared, being taken away from the only home he had ever known, poor little guy didn't know what was going on. When our trip was over, Matthew pulled into the driveway, reached over to pet Oliver and let him know what a good and brave boy he was and Oliver threw up in his hand. Aside from being removed from the comfort of such a loving home, it appeared that our new family member had motion sickness, and probably felt like throwing up all the way home. I got out of the car with Oliver in my arms and quickly unlocked the front door so that Matthew could wash his hands. I made Oliver a nice, cozy bed and he drifted off to sleep.

Those first few months were definitely a challenge. Just like a baby, a puppy can wear you out! They require a lot of time and patience, but it was worth it. Poodles are second on the intelligence chart of all dog breeds and Oliver was no exception. He learned very quickly to exit his doggy door to conduct his business, and he learned his basic commands of sit, stay, come and heel when he was on his leash, almost overnight. He had such an easy, mellow personality and he was very obedient. He was a little trooper who was willing to do *almost* anything we asked of him, but he found something in our home that he became infatuated with, an addiction if you will. Our sweet little bundle of joy was a vandal in disguise. While we were away at work, Oliver would vandalize our home by stringing toilet paper *through the inside and to the outside* by way of his doggy door. We would pick up his mess; he would put his head down, tuck his tail between his legs and briefly peek up at us to see if he was still in trouble.

In spite of his prior offenses and punishments, the little vandal would instantly perk up as he watched us pull out a fresh roll to replace that which he had destroyed, just a few moments earlier. He wanted his irresistible toy back; he loved it so much that the mere sight of it shattered his obedience compass and it was painfully obvious to us that he was going to do it again, and again, until we figured out how to train him out of his bad behavior.

It seemed like a simple fix; put the toilet paper away, or put Oliver where there was no toilet paper; either way we would have solved the problem. That solution seemed easy enough, as long as we didn't forget to put the rolls away, and we forgot on many occasions.

The scene was the same each time; we would pull into the driveway, open the front door, and there would be a paper mess strung out through the living room, into the kitchen and it would lead straight out the doggy door, and it would be strewn all over the back yard. This happened more times than I care to admit.

Dogs have a keen sense of what's going on inside of a person, and because of the repeated papering violations that took place in my home; I know that statement to be true. One afternoon, Matthew and I walked through the door into the familiar scene of a toilet paper path throughout the house that trailed through the doggy door.

In our mind's eye, we could see the carnage that awaited us in the back yard. I was expecting the instant replay where the little deviant would lower his head in shame, put his tail between his legs and wait to be scolded, but that day was different. Oliver must have sensed that Matthew's patience were stretched further than that roll of toilet paper, and all of the others combined because he took one look at Matthew, and bolted out the doggy door.

He somehow knew that his pitiful displays of shame, his seemingly heartfelt remorse, and fear filled eyes that seemed to shout, *I promise I will never do it again* would no longer earn him clemency. Matthew picked up all of the paper, rolled it into a ball, went outside and threw it on top of him and that was the end of Oliver's criminal mischief, his rap sheet was complete; Oliver was rehabilitated, and never did it again.

It wasn't long before Oliver became the hit of the neighborhood, he was so smart, loyal, athletic and handsome, and he was the reason that we became acquainted with all of our neighbors. When we took him on his walks, everyone wanted to meet him because he was so unique. We waited a long time to get a dog and our timing was perfect because it was obvious that Oliver was born to be ours.

The temp agency had placed me with a company as an Executive Assistant that required me to be on the computer for ninety-five percent of my day. I was nearing the end of my service for them, and as much as I enjoyed being there I was looking forward to it coming to an end because it was so hard on my eyes. On the other hand, it was so close to my home that I could visit Oliver on my lunch hour and on occasion I would take him back to the office with me because my boss enjoyed his presence. As my time at that job was coming to a close, I began to look for permanent work in the same area so I could continue my lunch time routine with Oliver. I was getting discouraged with my search; the next several interviews were unsuccessful. I just couldn't seem to find the right fit. At the end of the day, on the last day of my job as an Executive Assistant, my boss approached me, shook my hand and thanked me for my service. He asked me to do one final thing for him before I left, "Make me an appointment at the University of Washington Eye Institute."

Life works in mysterious ways. We follow paths that lead us in different directions for very specific reasons, without realizing that an exact moment in time is a moment we were meant to be in. Only in hindsight do we realize that there's something or someone controlling this universe that is incredibly powerful. Just one day later, I would not have been at that office and not been asked to call the University of Washington. I was meant to be there. I was not planning it, but after I made the appointment for my boss, the words just came out of my mouth and I made one for myself, a decision that would not only change the direction of my life, but would also dramatically change the role that Oliver would play in my life.

Chapter 8

WORLD RENOWNED

I was feeling excited as I sat in the waiting room of the UW Eye Institute. I had read about the eye doctors there, they were some of the best in the world. I had been under the care of great eye surgeons in the past, but something about that place made me feel a bit awestruck.

The first doctor I met was a surgeon who specialized in corneal and lens surgeries. She was compassionate, a great listener and obviously brilliant. She was the first surgeon to perform a corneal transplant in China; she gave a young man his sight for the first time in his life, and knowing I was being examined *by her*, was a great feeling. She explained to me, that although she specialized in lens problems, she had never seen a healthy person with two dislocated lenses. Because it was a University hospital, I was also examined by a couple of students. Word about me and my unique impairment spread through the institute like a wildfire and before I knew what was happening, there was a long line of doctors and students waiting outside of the exam room to take a look at me.

They told me my condition was so rare, that there was no number they could put on it, such as one in a million, because there wasn't another documented case that was like mine.

One of the first things that my surgeon wanted me to do was go through testing to determine if I had any of the genetic conditions that were normally associated with dislocated lenses. She sent me away with a list of tests to be completed by my family doctor, before she would see me again. Over the next month I had so much blood drawn, I felt like a pin cushion. All of the tests came back negative for any genetic conditions. It appeared that my eyes just didn't form property in the womb.

Having the tests done opened up Pandora's Box on my health. My heart had to be checked because one of the genetic problems associated with eye problems like mine included heart irregularities. Other than a slight murmur, my heart was healthy. They also tested my bone density and unfortunately, I was diagnosed with osteoporosis. I was too young to have that "silent disease" as they call it. Although that was very disappointing news, there was a part of me that was glad that I found out when I did so I could work hard to keep it from progressing.

More tests would follow at a later date, but they were satisfied at that point and could begin my eye care.

The next time I met with my surgeon she told me she felt it was in my best interest to see one of the top lens specialists in the country that she knew, he was in Cincinnati, Ohio. He had invented a lens ring and it was successful for many. He would sew the ring into the eye and place a new lens inside of the ring. Matthew and I talked it over and decided that it would be worth a trip to Ohio to see what that doctor had to say. Just a few weeks later I was sitting in his waiting room, feeling overwhelmed, while trying to remain optimistic.

After an exhausting 4 hour examination, he finally sat down to talk with me.

We discussed the results of all of the tests that had been performed on me that day. He told me that out of all the cases he had seen, mine was the most challenging. He explained that the lens ring wouldn't work for me because my lens structure wasn't strong enough to support the ring. He felt that the only thing that could possibly work would be to have my entire lens structure, including all of the weak ligaments taken out of my eyes and replaced with artificial lenses, and that he could perform the surgery.

What he said next was so nice, He said, "I could perform this surgery on you Linda, but if you were my sister, I would want you to have the surgery done close to home, not several hundred miles away."

He continued to say that he would discuss his findings and recommendations with my surgeons at the University of Washington.

I went back to my hotel room and collapsed on my bed. I felt completely exhausted and emotionally spent. I called Matthew with the disappointing news and he just quietly listened as I cried and expressed my fears about what was going to happen to my eyesight. I told him I was so scared that no one would ever be able to help me, and that one day my lenses would just drop into the back of my eyes and my vision would be gone for good.

It was beyond my comprehension that world renowned doctors were telling me that I was their most challenging case. Once my tears subsided, Matthew, as always, was able to comfort and reassure me everything would work out just fine. Considering the trauma I endured that day. I'm still not sure how I was able to sleep so well that night, I got on a plane the next morning and headed home to Washington.

When I returned to Washington, my surgeon at the University explained that before we could begin the process, I have would have to see the Vitreo Retinal surgeon because he was one of the best in the country, and he would be the one to start it. A few weeks later, Matthew and I were sitting in an exam room waiting to meet the man that could potentially change my life. He entered the room, closed the door behind him, sat down, looked at me and said, "Linda, I think I can help you and I will start with your right eye first.

"I will need to remove every part of your natural lens structure, and sew an artificial lens into your eye.

"I will go through the back of your eye, which will require me to work around the retina and remove the natural vitreous around it, which is called a vitrectomy.

"After I sew the new lens to your sclera (the white part of the eye), I will replace the vitreous gel that I had to take out."

He also told me, as with any surgery, there were risks. Some of those risks included trauma to the retina or other parts of the eye, bleeding in the eye, high eye pressure, among other things. He reassured me although there were risks; the chances of any of them happening were less than one percent. He said, "The result I expect will be the best vision you have ever had. I have an opening in my schedule in three weeks, would you like to schedule the surgery?"

Matthew and I were speechless. Out of everything that he said all I could think about were his first words, "Linda, I think I can help you."

I was so excited about that short little sentence that I started crying. I hugged Matthew and then I hugged the doctor. "Thank you, thank you" was all I could say to him. Boy did Matthew and I celebrate that night!

Chapter 9

"PATCHES"

The doctors had to be sure the lens they were implanting was the precise prescription. So prior to the surgery, the tests I had to go through were unreal and there were so many that I lost count. During one of the tests I was strapped onto a table that moved in many directions. Because my natural lens never stayed in one place, they had a very difficult time manipulating it to the center. At one point my head was pointing to the ground and my feet to the ceiling. That was the only way they could get my lens to float and stay in the correct position.

One week before my surgery, the kitchen gadget manufacturing company I had worked for years earlier called me. They heard I was looking for a new job and they wanted me back. My position would pretty much be the same as before, only better. I would be planning events and running the administrative functions for the sales department, and the best part was; I wouldn't have to supervise anyone. I was thrilled about the offer but had to explain that I was about to have major eye surgery and would not be able to start for about four weeks. They said that wasn't a problem, and they were willing to wait for me.

Three days before my operation was scheduled my surgeon called and said all of the doctors involved in my case had a meeting and decided that it would be best for the health of my eye if they removed my natural lens, and waited a little while to implant the artificial lens. He also explained that they wanted the eye to be completely healed before the implantation and he hoped that it would only take a few weeks.

I was a bit nervous since I was starting a new job. I had to stay positive and have faith that everything was going to be fine. I called my employer and explained my situation. I told them it was possible that I would need to start work at a slower pace because I would only be able to use one eye, and there would be another surgery that would follow within a few weeks after I started work. They were so kind and said they would support me one-hundred percent.

The surgery to remove the first lens was in June of 2004 and it went just fine. I only needed pain medication for a couple of days and felt fine, but it was extremely difficult trying to function with an eye that had no lens and the other eye that had a dislocated lens.

I felt sick to my stomach, dizzy, unbalanced, and had horrible headaches. I'm sure there were people who thought I was drunk because I walked into objects and walls. I had no choice but to cover the right lens of my glasses with a dark piece of paper because I could only see light and color with it. I was relying on my left eye, the best corrected vision I had with that eye was 20/50.

I felt embarrassed starting my new job with a black patch on my glasses, but I had no choice, so I walked into the office with my head held high. It was obvious that my co-workers were shocked at my appearance, but they understood and treated me with respect and kindness. Matthew called me "Patches" and told me how cute I was.

I went to the doctor every two weeks to have my eye examined to see if it was healed enough to have the next surgery, but there was a lot of swelling that just wouldn't go down. This went on week after week after week.

The persistent swelling in my eye, the anxiety from anticipating the next implant surgery, while struggling to keep up at work, was becoming unbearable. I was being stretched to my limits. Just when I didn't think I could take anymore my family doctor called and told me that he was contacted by the liver specialist about the results of one of the tests that he had done prior to my surgery. The same tests that I mentioned earlier, that opened up Pandora's Box. I had a spot on my liver that they wanted to biopsy—*Liver cancer?*

About a week later I had the biopsy, and they told me I would be fine to go back to work a couple of days later and I did, but I *was not* fine. I was sitting at a co-workers desk discussing a project and I started feeling so terrible that I called Matthew and he took me to the emergency room. They were able to quickly determine that nothing was seriously wrong. The area where the biopsy was done was just below my diaphragm and I was told to expect some discomfort for a few more days. I was also lucky enough to find that the results of the biopsy came back negative for cancer. I was flooded with relief when the doctor explained that the tissue was normal tissue, but there was an extra piece. He further explained that it was common for people to have an extra piece of liver tissue, but my extra piece looked different than anything he'd ever seen. I thought to myself, *well, of course it did, why wouldn't my liver have a rare appearance to go with my rare eye condition?* I was getting tired of being rare and unique.

Several weeks had passed and my prayers for the next surgery were intensified. Besides my increasing struggle to do my job, I had a very serious problem that I was keeping from Matthew. I was having difficulty seeing well enough to drive. Matthew would casually bring it up from time to time, but I felt I had no other choice to be a little less than honest with him because I needed my job, and I didn't want to lose my independence, so I would reassure him, "I'm fine behind the wheel, I can see just fine."

That little white lie would soon be revealed.

I can't remember exactly how many days had passed after I told Matthew that driving wasn't a problem for me, but soon after, I was at work, it was the end of the day, and I had lost track of time. I looked at the clock and was suddenly gripped with fear. I grabbed my purse and left the office, willing myself to run or even walk faster but I couldn't see well enough—I was in a race against daylight and I was in such a state of panic that I was having difficulty breathing. I prayed to God that I wouldn't get stuck in traffic and still be on the road after it was dark.

The traffic crawled at a snail's pace, as the sky began to darken. I thought about calling Matthew from my cell phone, but I didn't dare take my one eye off the road.

God answered my prayer in part, because I still don't understand how I made it home that night, but somehow there always seemed to be a car in front of me, and I followed the hazy red glow of tail lights, all the way home. I had just one more turn to make and it was onto my street. I was beginning to feel a little sense of relief, until I made the final turn into our home and saw Matthew's silhouette standing in the driveway. I couldn't see his face, but I could feel his worry, and it overwhelmed me with sadness and a sense of defeat. He opened my door, helped me out of the car and just held me without saying anything. My breathing was labored from the stress and the fear that had overcome me from driving in the dark. He finally broke the silence and said, "Linda, we need to talk."

We walked inside and Oliver greeted me with his tail wagging and sweet face looking up at me. I started petting him and talking to him, hoping to avoid the rest of the conversation with Matthew. I knew what he was going to say, but I didn't want to hear the words. He then said, "Linda, you need to give me your keys."

I started crying and held on tight to Oliver for comfort. I tried to reassure Matthew that I wouldn't let it happen again, and that I would never leave the office late, but it was useless; my pleas and promises didn't move him. When I realized that his mind was made up and there was nothing I could say to change it, I clutched the keys even tighter, walked across the room and turned away from him. Oliver could sense my unhappiness. He followed me across the room, got close enough to me to touch my leg, sat down and looked up at me with those sweet, loving eyes. I could feel his love for me and imagined what he would say to me if her were human and could talk.

Matthew said, "Linda, I realize how bad you want to make this work, but we both know that it's not safe for you to drive anymore."

"We will figure out a way to get you to and from work, and get everything else done until your eyes are fixed, it will be temporary."

He walked up behind me and gently took the keys out of my hand. He put his arms around me and held me as I wept.

Chapter 10

OVERLOAD

I believe there are many businesses that would have just let me go, but once again the company that I worked for accommodated me by allowing me to work the same hours as Matthew, and I was so grateful. Matthew had to take a different route to work, in order to drop me off and pick me up, day after day. Most days it worked out just fine but some days were awful. We were getting up much earlier every morning so that Matthew could get to work on time. On several occasions when Matthew would arrive to pick me up, I wasn't finished with what I was doing so he would have to wait for me.

In addition to working all day and driving me everywhere, Matthew was carrying the full load of our household chores. I had so little energy left at the end of each day, he had to do the grocery shopping, the housecleaning, pay the bills, do the yard work, and the laundry. He never made me feel bad, but I did, how could I not? He was exhausted, but he did his best to remain positive, cheerful and supportive. The days became so long for us and it was beginning to take its toll. My eyes were under tremendous strain and they hurt all the time. I was trying so hard to satisfy my employer and oftentimes it was at Matthew's expense, I felt so guilty. I was trying to take care of Oliver and my home while fighting off thoughts that I could end up blind if my eyes couldn't heal well enough to continue with the surgeries. I tried to stay hopeful and positive, but it didn't always keep that one devastating thought away, *if something doesn't happen for me soon will I have to live out the rest of my days in darkness?*

The strain and the pressures were so heavy and then Oliver became ill. He was only a year old and he began to lose his appetite on a regular basis. He was eating about half the amount of food he should have been, had diarrhea all of the time and would vomit every couple of days. His fun playful side was diminishing. Our veterinarian ran several tests and make suggestions to adjust his diet but he wasn't improving. He got so sick at one point, the diarrhea coming out of him was straight blood. I remember standing in the back yard, in the pouring rain, as my eye patch got soaking wet, crying, as I washed the blood out of the grass with the hose. I would go inside, dry myself and Oliver with a towel. I hugged, comforted and assured him I would do whatever it took to help him get better. I would sit at the table, peel the wet patch off of my glasses and replace it with a dry one. I was so weary, just so tired of the intense agony of the seemingly never-ending stream of disappointment around every single corner. The weight that was added from my sweet Oliver was so heavy; I was functioning in a state of numbness which prevented me from going into total despair. I chose numb, because surrender or defeat would never be an option.

We took Oliver to an internal medicine vet. The doctor did an endoscopy on him and discovered he had badly inflamed intestines. With his type of disease, there were only a handful of proteins he would be able to digest. We started him on intestinal medicine, started cooking buffalo meat and rice for him and dehydrated yams became his treats. He began to improve. From time to time he had flare ups, and eventually we had our happy, sweet boy back. You've never seen two happier people as we celebrated in the back-yard picking up solid, healthy poop!

Oliver's health was back on track, but the extra worry, expense and labor of feeding him made our challenging situation more difficult. I was being stretched to my limits. The weight of the load was getting heavier, and I felt my strength diminishing. I could feel myself becoming more stressed and overwhelmed with each day that passed. Every day was a fight to make it through but there were days when I felt that I wouldn't be able to hang on much lon-ger, and I didn't have the courage to admit it to Matthew; I didn't want to disappoint him. I was also afraid that if I couldn't find the strength to keep up the fight with a *"can do"* attitude, that it would somehow have a domino effect of *"can't do's"* in my life, and I couldn't even imagine what that would look or feel like, and I was afraid, I was petrified.

I don't think that my decision to have the lens implants would have been different had I known that I would have to wait four months instead of two weeks in-between surgeries, but it wasn't what I ex-pected and it wasn't something that I was prepared for. Summer was passing, Fall was in the air, the leaves were turning beauti-ful colors of red, orange and yellow but along with fall, came the cold, the dark mornings, the dark afternoons and the relentless Washington rain, that seemed to compound and exaggerate every-thing that I was feeling; I was physically and emotionally drained and I yearned for relief.

One night on our way home from work, Matthew and I stopped at the grocery store. We were strolling through the produce aisle and I began to laugh. Matthew chuckled and said, "What is so funny?"

I couldn't answer him because my laughter became hysterical, out of control and I couldn't stop it. I mean I really couldn't stop it, and the worst part was; I didn't feel happy. It wasn't happy laughter, and in my effort to compose myself I began sobbing uncontrollably. The sobs would turn to laughter, and then the laughter back to sobs and the cycle repeated itself over and over. Once Matthew realized that I wasn't able to control what was happening to me, he abandoned the shopping cart and all of its contents, and quickly ushered me to the car. As we drove home I broke out in a sweat and felt sick to my stomach. Matthew tried his best to calm and reassure me that everything was going to be okay, and every fiber of my being wanted to believe that what he was saying was true. We came to a harsh reality that night; we both knew that there was no way that I could continue on like I had been all summer long. Something had to change, and it had to change fast.

I mentioned earlier in the book; perfect timing, perfect places and perfect things happening in our lives, and I can't say that it was perfect timing but I can say that it came *just in time*; the phone call that I received from my doctor just two-days after my breakdown, "Hello Linda, it's time to have the lens implanted."

I felt so relieved when I heard those words—I was ecstatic!

The lens implant surgery that was performed by my female surgeon took place in October of 2004, four months after my natural lens was removed, and was the most painful of all the surgeries I had went through, or ever would go through. I wasn't much of a drinker, so when the anesthesiologist asked me how many drinks it took to get me drunk, I told her one or two. I should have said four or five because she gave me just enough anesthesia to make my eye feel numb, and hinder me from speaking. I felt an intense pulling and dull heavy pain in my eye with every move the surgeon made. I couldn't form the words to tell her how much pain I was feeling, all I could do was moan. Finally, she figured out what I was trying to tell her. At that point all she could do was administer numbing drops every couple of minutes to keep the pain down, which helped very little considering she was using a needle to sew a lens into my eye. She tried to comfort me and talk me through it. The surgery lasted about one hour, to me it felt like a year.

In the beginning it appeared that the surgery was a success. I was excited and felt so positive about the future. I was told that my vision wouldn't be good immediately following the surgery, but we remained optimistic that as the swelling went down, I would see better each day and it wouldn't be long before I had my life back.

If only it could have gone that way...

Chapter 11

LESS THAN ONE PERCENT

My doctors predicted that my eye would heal very quickly. They suggested that I take one week off from work and said I could resume the rest of my normal activities in approximately two weeks. A few days passed and my eye struggled to heal. The lens was tilting and was rubbing the iris, which caused swelling and bleeding on the inside of the eye and I wasn't able to see anything out of it. Three days after the surgery I woke up in terrible pain, my eye was throbbing, it had hardened up, I was vomiting and I was so off balance, I could barely walk.

Matthew called my doctors and they told him to bring me in right away, because my symptoms indicated high eye pressure, which could damage the optic nerve and lead to blindness.

Matthew practically had to carry me to the car. I was so sick to my stomach that I held a bowl in my lap in the car. The thirty minute drive to the University felt like an eternity, I was in so much pain. When I arrived, the doctors rushed me into the exam room and took my eye pressure; it was at forty eight! Normal eye pressure should be in the low to mid-teens. I was in a very dangerous range so they had to act quickly. As the doctors were getting everything together, I was in the exam chair with poor Matthew sitting in front of me holding the bowl. When the vomiting would stop for a few minutes, I was given medications that would remove fluid from the eye, and hopefully lower the eye pressure. First they gave me pills, and then they gave me sixteen ounces of a drink that was sickeningly sweet and very thick. It tasted like a flat Mountain Dew with a bottle of syrup added to it! It was hard to keep it down, but somehow I was able to. The medications acted quickly, the vomiting stopped and my eye pressure slowly came down. They couldn't get the pressure down to normal levels but were able to stabilize it in the mid twenties, which is just below the danger zone so they sent me home with drops that would keep the pressure down. I don't remember the ride home, or Matthew putting me to bed.

My next post-op appointment was scheduled for one week later. I was able to go back to work the following week, but I had to take it slow. I was able to get a little bit of work done, but unfortunately I was still not able to use the right eye. At my next appointment, my doctor agreed that the visible parts of my eye were healing very well, but what was going on inside my eye was a much different story. The lens was still rubbing the iris and the eye was holding onto blood and fluid. My eye pressure was trying to reach thirty, so I was given a mild dose of eye pressure medication again. I was not physically ill, but I felt a constant dull throbbing in my eye. My doctor sent me home with more eye pressure drops and told me to return in one week.

I didn't make it to the one week appointment; I was back at the UW just a few days later at ten o'clock at night with pain in my eye, and all I could see was white. The fluid had built up again and the pressure went up to the high thirties. The resident working that night was very nice but she had never treated me before. I had been through it so many times, so I knew she was following the proper protocols. She examined me, and called my surgeon. As I listened to her conversation with him, she seemed confident and it appeared that she understood what to do, so when she handed me the pills and the awful drink, I thought nothing of it, until the drink was almost gone, and then I realized that the consistency was different and it tasted much sweeter than it did before. I casually mentioned it to her, but we were all so concerned about getting it in me that we didn't discuss it any further.

I could feel the medicine working right away, almost too quickly. I felt very strange all the way to the car. As we were pulling out of the parking lot, I started to feel extremely weak. Suddenly, a sharp, horrible pain shot through my head and through my chest. Matthew quickly turned the car around and took me into the university's hospital emergency center.

As we made our way into the building, I could barely walk or speak. I was incoherent and I was freezing. I felt as though I was having a heart attack, and felt like I was going to die. I had my face buried in Matthew's chest because I couldn't stand to have my eyes open. I was trying so hard to tell Matthew how much I loved him and to please take good care of Oliver because I didn't think I was going to live much longer and I was trying to say goodbye, but I could barely speak.

Matthew was frantically trying to explain to the doctors and nurses what transpired moments earlier at the eye center. He told them they needed to call the resident so that she could explain what medication I had been given. They contacted my doctor and it was explained to us that I been "sucker punched" by the medicine. The dosage she gave me was too strong and I was experiencing an overdose. My entire body had become completely dehydrated from the medication, it definitely brought the eye pressure down, but it almost killed me in the process!

I was covered in warm blankets, given IV fluids and the doctor informed me that he was giving me morphine for the pain. He asked me if I knew anything about morphine. The only thing I knew about morphine was from watching an episode of, Little House on the Prairie where Albert became addicted to it. I was already in "la la land" and I said, "Yes I know all about morphine, I watch Little House on the Prairie."

Matthew said he and the doctor just smiled at me, I heard someone giggling from the nurses and that's the last thing that I remember about that night.

After dozens of emergency visits to the eye center and my near death experience, my eye started to show small signs of improvement. My eye pressure had remained stable in the low to mid-twenties for two weeks. Needless to say, it was difficult for me at work. The pressure medications made me very tired and my eye constantly hurt. I was starting to think that I may not be able to stay at my job. I was trying so hard to remain optimistic about the outcome of my surgery. I really believed my eye would heal soon and all would be well. I wanted so much to heal, be successful at work and enjoy my life again. My doctors told me they had rarely seen traumas like this in anyone. The traumas I was going through had happened to less than one percent of their other patients. In order to make me feel better, they would smile and tell me I was rare and very special, and that they believed everything would be fine.

The physical and emotional roller coaster we were on was hard enough, but we were starting to hurt financially also. We paid a copay for every single visit to the UW. The copays were more than normal because the UW was considered a "facility" rather than a doctor's office. There was a period of time in November that I had to go in and see them, ten days in a row. From October through December we paid nearly a thousand dollars in copays. In addition to the copays, we were dishing out a lot of money on medications, gas and parking as a result of all of the trips we made to the university.

When we weren't in the midst of an emergency, we were lucky to have good friends that we enjoyed spending time with. We had some really good times, they kept us laughing, and laughter is definitely the best medicine. Those friends know who they are and we are grateful to them.

Through everything, Matthew and I had to remain hopeful and positive. We were going through such a difficult time, but we just weren't willing to be depressed or give up.

When I felt good enough, I would exercise and it was extremely helpful. It made my mind and body feel much better. My time with Oliver was incredibly helpful too. He always stayed very close to me; he knew I was going through a tough time.

When Oliver and I weren't spending time together at home, we would take long walks. Somehow Oliver instinctively knew how to help me with my balance and depth perception problems without even being taught. As we walked he would use his body to keep me from running into things, or to keep me walking straight. It only took him one time of seeing me trip on a curb for him to understand that he needed to be proactive, and alert me.

He seemed to be keenly aware of when I needed him most. When I was feeling really down and out, he would simply walk up to me and let me wrap my arms around his soft furry neck and hug him. He would lay his head on my shoulder as if he was hugging me back in an effort to console me.

There was no doubt in my mind that Oliver was brought into my life at just the right time.

Chapter 12

"I'll Get to Hold Your Hand"

We went to my weekly appointment one afternoon, and my doctor explained that my retina had been badly traumatized throughout the ordeal. The retina had become very swollen and inflamed and was in danger of detaching, which would cause blindness. He explained that he needed to get medication into the back of my eye, to the retina, right away. He leaned me back in the chair, propped my eye open and proceeded to stick the needle into my eye. He was very quick with the injection. The discomfort, which was an intense feeling of pressure, only lasted about 4 seconds and he was done. As the medication was going in, I saw nothing but blackness for a few seconds. The anxiety and fear that I experienced prior to the injection was much worse than the actual injection itself, and it took a toll on my body. Matthew took me home, put me to bed, and again, I slept for a long, long time. Luckily the shot in my eye took place on a Friday because it took the entire weekend for my body to recover from the stress.

We were looking forward to Christmas which was only a couple of weeks away. As I rested and recovered that weekend, I could tell something was not right with my eye. At the bottom of my eye I could see a large black spot, I called the office and the resident on duty explained that the black spot was probably normal but to let them know if it persisted.

The next day the black spot was still there and growing larger, I knew something was wrong. I called in again and was told to come in right away. The assistant surgeon on staff that night was a woman who I never did care for. She had a terrible bedside manner and was a horrible communicator. She was very cold and abrupt and I didn't have a lot of confidence in her. She always had the same outfit on, a long, black blouse, black gaucho type pants and black high heeled boots. When she walked by she reminded me of the wicked witch in the Wizard of Oz.

The resident that was working that night was wonderful; I had seen him a few times. The wicked witch was being very rude to him. I spoke up and said "Hey, I like him more than any of the resident doctors here, and you need to be nice!" She didn't say another word and left the room. He examined me, and went out in the hall to call my surgeon. He came back into the exam room, and as sweetly and as gently as possible, he went behind me and lowered the back of the exam chair so that I was lying flat.

He sat beside me, held my hand, and told Matthew and I that my retina was torn and I would be going into emergency surgery. I began to cry, he had tears in his eyes too.

Matthew walked over to me and held me. I said, "I'm so afraid Matthew, what if I go blind?"

He said, "You don't need to be afraid because I love you and I will always be here.

"I don't believe that you're going to go blind, but if you do, I'll just get to hold your hand all the time."

I was taken to the emergency surgery unit where my surgeon was waiting for me, and he looked heartbroken.

I could tell by his sad expression that his next words were some of the most difficult words that he had ever spoken, "Linda, I am so sorry.

"It looks like when I gave you the injection the other day; the needle went through the sclera and tore your retina.

"I think the tear is small and I am confident that I can easily repair it.

"We will have to wait a few days after the surgery to determine if any permanent damage has been done to the retina.

"We are going to give you general anesthesia for this surgery and you will be in the hospital for a day or two.

"When you wake up, you will be lying face down so that the retina can stabilize."

He smiled sadly and said, "I'll see you when you wake up."

I have never been a stomach sleeper and waking up that way was not enjoyable. I was lying face down with my head resting in something similar to a massage table head rest. I was only able to move to go to the bathroom or to have something quick to eat and drink.

I told Matthew to go home and get some sleep, I didn't want him to stay there all night and become exhausted, plus he needed to take care of Oliver. He went home and rested as best as he could, and he was there sitting beside me when I woke up. He told me when he laid down in our bed that night; he was praying for me with all that he had in him, he said he also said a prayer for himself. My heart ached as I considered the totality of what he had been through and how much he'd endured.

I was examined by my doctor and was released to go home the next day, and was told that I would have to sleep sitting up for about five days. Even though we had a very comfortable recliner, five days of that was more than enough! We had a very quiet Christmas that year.

My first post-op appointment with my surgeon was difficult. I knew it was not good when my eye patch came off. He and Matthew and I were all very sad to discover that there was damage to the retina, I was now completely blind peripherally and also in the upper area of my eye.

As I recovered at home, luckily I could still watch television with my left eye to pass the time. I had several favorite shows, but one day I found myself watching another episode of Little House on the Prairie. The actor, Michael Landon, was talking to his wife about the illness their daughter was going through. She said she had been praying that God would heal her and she couldn't understand why she wasn't getting better. He said to her, "Maybe you're not praying for the right thing, maybe you need to pray for the strength to get through whatever happens."

That was a defining moment for me. I had been praying for my eyes to get better, so I could see well. I knew I still had a long road ahead of me and that I may never see well again. That day I began to pray for the strength to get through whatever was to come my way. I felt an immediate surge of strength come over me that very moment, a strength that would carry me through the days, weeks, months and years ahead.

Chapter 13

DENIED

As I recovered at home, it was very obvious to both Matthew and I that I would have to stop working for a while. My eye needed time to rest and heal, and so did I. I knew I couldn't give my employer one hundred percent.

I loved my job and it broke my heart to leave it, but I was exhausted and needed to let go. As usual, they were so gracious and understanding. They knew what I had been going through and they expressed to me that all they cared about was that I healed and felt better. I knew I would probably not be able to go back to work there, but I remember thinking it would be exciting to start something new when both of my eyes were healed and my new implanted lenses were giving me good vision. Even though I had lost a lot of vision in the right eye because of the upper and peripheral blindness, I remained hopeful about the final outcome.

The repair to my retina was successful but the implanted lens would not stabilize. We continued to struggle with dangerously high eye pressure throughout all of January and February.

In March of 2005, my surgeon gave me that sad look again and said, "I'm sorry Linda, but it's become clear that your eye isn't going to tolerate the implanted lens.

"We cannot allow your eye to continue being traumatized this way.

"We all feel it would be in your best interest if we removed the implant.

"Unfortunately, this will leave you with very poor vision in your right eye.

"We can't predict anything at this time, but we think that your eye should heal well enough that we will eventually be able to fit you for a contact lens."

I said, "Okay, I understand, but what about my left eye, what will we do about that dislocated lens?"

He replied, "We'll have to deal with that down the road, right now we want to concentrate on getting your right eye out of danger."

My wonderful implanted lens that was supposed to change my life was being taken out and there was no hope of ever getting it back. My surgery was scheduled for one week later.

All of the doctors and nurses had come to know me pretty well. I was now having my 4th surgery with them in eight months. They all told me they looked forward to what silly thing I was going to say while I was being given my anesthesia.

On that particular day, they asked me to tell them my birth date, I did, and my surgeon said, "Hey, that's my birthday".

My surgeon and I were born on the same day, only hours apart! It took four surgeries to discover that! Then they asked me if there was anything else I wanted to say. I said yes and before I went under, I started to sing "supercalifragilisticexpialidocious," from Mary Poppins. I heard a lot of laughter, and the next thing I knew I was waking up in recovery.

It only took a few weeks to realize getting that artificial lens out of my eye was the best thing ever! My eye pressure went back to normal levels and physically I felt much better. I couldn't see a damn thing out of that eye, but I felt better!

The sad reality was that I was legally blind in my right eye. Legal blindness is when the vision cannot be corrected to 20/200. They didn't give me an exact number at that time because my vision was so distorted. All I could see was light and color. Everyone and everything looked like a blob of whatever color it was. Humans looked like colored ghosts, it was very strange. I couldn't stand to use both eyes at the same time so I continued to wear glasses with a patch on the right side. The best corrected vision I was getting with my left eye was 20/60.

Matthew and I knew that I wouldn't be able to go back to work again for a long time, if ever. My right eye was far from recovered and my left eye could not carry the load. I decided to apply for Social Security Disability benefits. That income wouldn't come close to what I was earning, but it would be better than nothing. We were paying our bills with Matthew's income, but there was nothing left over, and we still had many medical expenses. I submitted my disability paperwork to the Social Security Administration and hoped to hear soon that I was approved.

I waited ten months to be told that I wouldn't be approved for disability. They had all of my medical records and all of my doctors explained that the vision in my left eye was not good enough to keep me working, and that my vision situation was very unpredictable and I could be facing more surgeries. It was clear that my twenty-eight years of working and contributing to Social Security didn't matter.

I got some good advice from a few experts, which I wished I had gotten the first time around. I hired a disability attorney and he filed an appeal for me. They told me there was a better chance I would win my case, but still no guarantees because the system was so broken. We did everything they asked. I was required to go through numerous tests with two eye specialists that Social Security required me to be examined by. Both doctors came back with the same diagnosis as my doctors and told Social Security that I should be approved for disability.

In early 2006, I was denied again. We were all in shock. The representative at the Social Security said to me, "Yes, our doctors indicated that you should receive your disability, however, the people in our office still do not agree."

I said, "So, the people sitting behind a desk in your office decided it didn't matter what the medical professional, who you hired, said"

She said, "Yes ma'am, that is correct."

The disbelief and anger inside of me was overwhelming. It was hard for me to wrap my mind around the stupidity and unfairness of it all. Somehow Matthew and I were making it financially, but just barely.

My attorney was just as frustrated as I was, but not surprised. He went into disability law because he saw so many deserving people, like me, being denied, while others were receiving disability that didn't deserve it, people that were cheating the system. He refused to give up on me, he filed a second appeal.

"Next time, "He said, "We're putting you in front of a judge."

As the disability fight dragged on, my eye pressure was normal but the retina was struggling. I had to have a second injection, and luckily there was no retina tear that time. In rare instances, in less than 10% of patients, a film called a "membrane" will form and tighten over the retina. The membrane will pull on the retina and can detach it, so it must be removed, and of course, I developed one. In early 2006, I had to have a 5th surgery; it was called a, "membrane peel." Every time my eye and body would start to recover, I had to go in for another surgery.

The membrane peel went well, and again, I was recovering. My eye would heal, as best as it could after each surgery. I learned that the eye is one of the bodies' fastest healing organs, but my body was a different story. My proprioception was a mess, which means that my balance was off; the distortion in my retina caused the world to look crooked. All of the blurry human beings I would see appeared to be walking with their bodies leaning to one side. My left eye was exhausted from doing all of the work.

Because of the financial struggles we were facing, we had to find ways to save money. It was painfully obvious that I would not drive again for a long time, if ever. My car was paid off but we still had payments on Matthew's. I loved my car, it was a beautiful 1996, 2-door Toyota Camry. The paint color was called "Ruby Pearl," and that's what I named her. My sister's car was in bad shape, so it worked out perfectly for her to buy my car. With that money we were able to pay off Matthew's car.

We drove Ruby Pearl to California to deliver her to my sister. I loved the time that I was able to spend with my sister and her family, but when it was over and we were standing at the airport watching her drive away in the last thing that gave me some sort of independence, it was tough. First it was my work, then my keys and finally the car. By the age of forty five, I had relinquished it all.

Chapter 14

JUST DANCE

I had fallen several times and all the muscles in my body were hurting. I went from one problem to the next; foot problems, knee problems and back problems. The medical costs were outrageous because I needed so much physical therapy, massage and chiropractic care. I was at an appointment with my female eye surgeon one day and out of the blue she asked me, "How is your back feeling?"

I couldn't believe she asked me that. I told her, "Not very good."

I explained all I had been going through physically and she wasn't surprised. She said it was common for those things to happen when the eyes go through severe trauma. Although I hated all I was experiencing, it felt so good to be validated that way. To be reassured I was not imagining the problems, was so helpful.

I would not allow my discomfort to keep me from exercising. I knew I had to keep my body as strong as possible. I would walk with Oliver, we had an exercise bike, and I would dance.

I loved music and I loved to dance. I didn't need good eyesight to dance, as long as all obstacles were out of the way. I would turn the music up loud and just dance, sometimes crying my eyes out as I moved to the beat of the music, and I would pray out loud asking God to give me the strength to keep on fighting. I refused to let my body shut down; I knew that I had to keep moving. The positive effects of the release of endorphins that came from exercise helped me immensely.

I was doing the best that I could to stay busy at home, but I really needed to get some independence back and get around somehow. It wasn't safe for me to leave the house alone, so I worked for the next few months training Oliver to be my service dog.

I had worked as an obedience and protection dog trainer many years earlier. Oliver was so intelligent and easy to train, he practically taught himself! He was already assisting me with walking, stepping off curbs and avoiding obstacles. I needed to teach him how to look both ways for cars, help me manage stairs, and go through distraction training. Oliver was certified as my service dog in early 2007. That was one of the best days ever!

I decided to be brave and venture out on the bus. Oliver and I started out in our local area first, and each time we left the house we would venture out a little further. Within a few months we were using the bus for transportation to run all of our errands and just explore when Matthew wasn't able to drive us.

Most days, I didn't have anywhere specific to go, but we still went out, rain or shine. We would go to my eye appointments and walk around the campus of the university. We would walk around downtown Seattle, sit and people watch and go into quaint cafes and have lunch. Sometimes we would go to a park and sit on a bench and just look at the beautiful surroundings. I would take him to dog parks and let him run and play. It really helped to get some independence back and be out in the world again. Not only was Oliver helping me visually, he was also keeping me safe.

Standard Poodles are sweet and gentle, unless you mess with their master! They are very protective. On a few occasions Oliver had to show his tough side to potential bad guys. While Oliver and I were waiting at a bus stop, two very stupid guys learned the hard way what not to do. They were walking up the sidewalk towards us, and started doing a "creepy walk" and saying, "Oooooohhhhh" to both of us. That was a big mistake. I knew that Oliver felt I was being threatened. I gave him some extra lead on his leash just in case I needed to jump away from the situation. He growled, barked his deep ferocious bark and lunged at them sending them out into the busy street. They nearly got run over! They were like two scared little boys. They were saying over and over how sorry they were while they ran away! He continued to bark at them until they were out of earshot.

Another time Oliver showed his fearless and protective side was while we were waiting in line for a bus at a transit center. There were four boys hanging out, who were up to no good and had been causing trouble there for weeks. Oliver spotted them immediately and kept a very close eye on them. He remembered them and he could spot trouble-makers a mile away. There were about a dozen people in line, and Oliver and I were in the middle. Suddenly those boys started walking towards us. As they got closer, it was apparent they were not going to walk *around* the line of people, they were intending on walking *through* it, right where Oliver and I were standing. Oliver's demeanor changed, his body stiffened up and then he tugged slightly on the leash. He turned his body so that he was facing them, and he had the most intimidating, tough stance I had ever seen, and I could hear a low growl coming from him. I couldn't see his eyes, but I knew they were piercing. He didn't move a muscle and stared those punks down! Needless to say, they decided to go around the line. A lot of people that were standing in that line were scared and nervous and unsure of what those boys were going to do. Everyone was so relieved when it was over. They were all telling Oliver what a good boy he was, while they thanked him. It was awesome; I was a very proud Mom.

Oliver and I had many fun, unique and exciting adventures together taking the bus. *I will cherish those memories forever.*

A few months later, in 2007, another membrane formed over my retina. Surgery number six was scheduled. We had developed a very close bond with my surgeon. Matthew and I would have long conversations with him. The prior three years had become so ridiculous and unbelievable, all we could do was make jokes and laugh about it. We discovered something else we had in common with him. He had grown up raising Standard Poodles. He loved the breed and he adored Oliver.

The second membrane peel was successful but because my sclera (the white part of the eye) was so thin, the stitches were not holding, which caused the fluid to come out of my eye; my eye pressure was at one! That was a very dangerous number because no fluid in the eye is just as dangerous as too much fluid. Both can damage the eye and cause blindness.

He was about to take me into emergency surgery when we decided to talk to my other surgeon. She put a huge, soft contact lens in my eye that covered nearly my entire eyeball. It sealed the sides where the stiches were coming loose and allowed my eye to regain the correct amount of fluid and my pressure went up to normal levels in a few hours.

I wore that contact for a couple of weeks, and slowly but surely, my retina and the rest of my eye stabilized. I still wore my patch and continued to rely on the left eye because they were still unable to make a contact for me. I continued my exercise and physical therapies. I knew there was a good possibility I would never see out of that eye again, but I remained cautiously optimistic.

Shortly after the last surgery, I was finally granted a disability hearing before a judge. He asked me a lot of questions and asked me to explain my condition to him. He asked his employment expert to determine what, if any job I could hold with my limitations. The expert explained that out of several hundred jobs in his database, there was not one job I could perform safely or reliably because of my eye condition. The judge treated me with respect and compassion. He wasn't able to tell me his decision that day, but my attorney, Matthew and I could tell he was shocked that I had been denied twice before. He said I would have his decision within a few weeks.

The judge kept his word, and three weeks later I received a big brown envelope from the Social Security Administration. I handed the envelope to Matthew because I was too afraid to open it. The words we were looking for were "favorable decision". Matthew read those words to me, telling me that after nearly three years of fighting and waiting, I had finally won my disability case! My legs became weak, and I collapsed to the floor, crying happy tears. I would receive my Social Security Disability payment every month for as long as I was unable to work. It wasn't a lot of money but, it felt like a million dollars to us! Matthew and I called my parents and the rest of our family to tell them the good news. That was also one of the best days ever!

I was given some back pay from Social Security. After using some of it to pay important bills, we took a much needed break from everything and went to Hawaii. I only had one low vision eye to see it with, but that was fine. Hawaii is always beautiful. When I was struggling to see something, Matthew was really good at describing things to me in vivid detail.

We really earned and needed that vacation, and we had a blast!

Chapter 15

MY PROMISE

*M*y name is Matthew. In December, 1990, I made a promise. It was a promise that has been made millions of times throughout history by millions of people. I promised my bride that I would love and cherish her for the rest of my life; through good times and bad, in sickness and in health. I'm not sure how many people understand the true gravity of those words when bad times become real time, sickness seeps in or how a tragedy of any kind could be waiting in your future to challenge everything that you're made of, as it alters your dreams and redirects the path of your well thought out journey of life. Those vows are easy to make, accept and look forward to, because happiness, joy, setting and reaching new goals are what you naturally envision as you make a promise of such great importance to someone that you love. The disappointment of not reaching those goals and things not going the way you planned is the reason why such an important commitment is too often broken.

I've been married to Linda for twenty three years, and I understand that every marriage is tested at some point and bonds just like promises get easily brushed aside, and often times for very insignificant reasons. Not only am I proud that I've kept my promise to Linda, it makes me happy to say that I've kept my promise to Linda despite all of the difficulties, disappointments, and sorrow of watching her suffer so much trauma, endure so much pain, and remain as positive as she possibly could facing so much uncertainty, so many times; it's been easy to keep my promise to Linda, and here's why:

The day started out pretty much the same as it did the previous several months. My co-worker and I were waist deep in a large hole that we were carving out of the hard-packed desert clay. It was the off-season at a waterpark, and I worked on the maintenance crew. I'd only been out of the Navy for about five months and was enjoying my new life after being in the military. Even though I was working my butt off doing manual labor, every day was filled with the promise of my future. My buddy and I were working away with a pick and shovel, when a subtle movement caught our eye. It was Linda, shouting to us because she needed directions to the office where she had an appointment to interview for the office manager position. We were about twenty-five yards away from her, she was easy to look at so, of course, we stood and watched her until she disappeared into the office. My buddy and I both were hoping that she would land the position—and lucky for me she did!

Linda fit in well with the off-season crew. We all got along well and enjoyed our days working together. A few weeks after she started we were all supposed to go to lunch together. Everyone changed their mind that morning for one reason or another except for Linda and I. Although this part was told by Linda earlier in the book, I'll tell it again, because it helps set the stage for our life together. We went to a sandwich shop that took phone orders in advance. Linda and I ordered separately, when we got there and sat down to eat our food, we had ordered the *exact* same sandwich. The more we talked the more we discovered that we had many other likes and dislikes in common. Linda obviously felt comfortable with me because she dropped a bombshell on me that day. She told me she was separated from her husband and about to divorce. Although I found her very attractive, I didn't allow myself to think about her romantically because I thought she was happily married until then. That bit of news changed things. I didn't know what would become of our relationship, but I knew I really liked her and wanted to get to know her better.

One of the things we both liked to do was hike, so we planned a hiking trip for the following week. The hike was great and we spent a great deal of the time talking and really getting to know one another. We enjoyed each other so much we made a date to go dancing the following weekend. I wish I could have pushed a fast-forward button and skipped right past that work week, the anticipation of being with her again was killing me. As I was getting ready for the evening, I wondered if I would kiss her that night, I kissed her, and a whole lot more. That was the night we became a couple.

The next day we went to the beautiful red rock country of Sedona. On the drive back we were commenting on the beauty of what we had just seen. I said to Linda that I thought we would see a lot of beautiful things together, but what I really meant was that I wanted to spend the rest of my life with her. I had been casually dating a very nice girl prior to meeting Linda and the first thing I did when we arrived back in Phoenix that day was meet with her to inform her that I could no longer date her. She took it well, I knew she was dating other guys and we didn't feel a strong enough connection to ever consider marriage, since we looked at our futures and saw very little in common. I told her that I had unexpectedly met the woman I was going to marry. In retrospect, it's funny that she was the first person I told that I wanted to marry Linda.

It all happened so fast and Linda wasn't even divorced. We both knew what we felt for each other and we both knew that our friends and family would probably have difficulty understanding our intense feelings, having spent so little time together. We tried to keep it a secret at work, but it didn't take long for our co-workers to figure out how we felt about each other.

Steve had been my best friend since high school, worked with me at the waterpark and we lived in apartment's right next to each other, so keeping it a secret from him would have been next to impossible, plus I have never liked keeping things from people that I was close to. When I told Steve that Linda and I were a couple he exclaimed, "Matt, she's married!" Even though he trusted me and my judgment, I think it took a while before he really believed it was a good idea for us to be together. There were many others that didn't take it so well and we were criticized to our face and behind our backs. It didn't matter what others thought, we knew it was right and we were married in less than ten months. That was the beginning of our bond. We faced scrutiny right from the start, but it didn't change our path. Neither one of us could imagine life without the other. We had to be together.

We started life the same as most young couples. We were poor and uncertain about the future, but excited for the possibilities. I left the waterpark shortly after meeting Linda to search for a better, higher paying job. I made a couple brief stops before starting a career with the federal government less than a year after our wedding. I had a conversation with my father shortly after getting out of the Navy. I told him that the next decade of my life was extremely exciting because I would probably meet the woman I was going to marry and find the job or career that

I would hold most of my life. I couldn't have been more right, but I never would have guessed that it would all happen in only two years.

Linda and I were living the American dream. We began to make a decent living, bought a house and had two cars in the garage, one of them new. We were going places, seeing all those beautiful things I had predicted and we were building our bond stronger and stronger. We worked as a team and set goals that we both could strive for. When I would hear people say that marriage was hard I felt sorry for them. My marriage to Linda had never been hard. We didn't agree on everything one hundred percent of the time, but we never fought. We certainly laughed a lot over the years and we hugged a lot, too. I didn't realize it at the time, but that sweet life we lived was building the strength that would be required for us to survive what awaited us in our future.

I knew my promotion potential in Arizona was minimal, so I took advantage of the opportunity to transfer to Seattle and off we went on a new adventure. It didn't take long for us to realize that Seattle wasn't the Disneyland experience we were expecting. Although the Pacific Northwest is undoubtedly one of the most beautiful places on earth, that beauty comes at a high price. Rain! Rain, rain and more rain! And worse than the rain were the clouds. Thick, grey clouds, that turn day into night. I was ready to quit my career and move back to the sunshine and do anything for a living. We took a deep breath and learned to live for the short, but oh so sweet summers that were the best in the world. We continued to travel and see beautiful things, both in the state as well as out of state trips to sunny locations. Linda started having more problems with her eyes and we wanted to see if the doctors could do something to help her, and that's when the promise I made when I said my wedding vows to Linda would start being tested.

Our painful experiences paled in comparison to what some people go through. We've experienced the deaths of close family members, financial challenges and career disappointments just to name a few. Add these things to what Linda has described in the many chapters before this one and you begin to see a glimpse of what we have endured. Through all the challenges, pain, suffering and disappointment, our love and support of each other has never waivered. It's difficult to watch a person that you love so much go through so much pain and suffering. Linda's suffering was both physical and mental, and I suffered along with her. I was her rock when she needed someone strong to lean on and she was mine when I needed her. Many years after the difficult times started Linda asked me a question that broke my heart. She must have been wondering if things were ever going to get better. I know she was feeling guilty that life was not going the way we thought it would after years of hard work and living within our means. I knew that she felt it was all her fault, the day she asked me, "Why do you keep me around?" I wanted to cry as my answer came quickly and from my heart. I responded, "Because I love you."

I'm proud to say that I've kept my promise. Life has not always been easy, but loving my wife has been.

Chapter 16

WINDOWS ROLLED DOWN

*W*hen we got home from Hawaii, we were relaxed, tanned and very happy to be home with our sweet boy, Oliver. Our wonderful friend and neighbor took care of him while we were away. We thought he was going to wag the puff off the end of his tail when we got home!

I took Oliver to the vet for a checkup. He had been doing pretty well but not great on his buffalo diet, not to mention, the cost of it was really hard to manage. The vet decided it would be a good time to try a new hypo allergenic dog food made with soy protein. We started Oliver on the new dog food and he loved it. Within a few weeks, his stool had improved dramatically and he began to have more energy. The cost savings for us each month was fantastic, too.

Life actually started to feel a bit normal again. We had hoped the extra money from my disability would help us breathe a little easier financially, but physically I was such a mess, the majority of it went towards medical bills, but we were thankful we had it. In 2008, there were no eye surgeries, which was wonderful! My body, however, had been through so much; I was in some type of physical therapy almost constantly. I had successes and then I would have setbacks.

In early 2009, Matthew, my surgeon and I were talking about how my body had been affected and what I was experiencing. He suggested it might be time to remove the lens from my left eye. We would not attempt to implant another artificial lens, but he believed, and I agreed with him, that if my eyes had similar vision, it would help me with my physical problems. The decision was not hard for me to make, I yearned to feel better and stronger. I knew there was a high possibility I may never be able to have my vision corrected in either eye. I needed to prepare myself that I would be legally blind in both eyes.

I could not continue with the way I was living, I knew I had to take the risk. I knew I had my Oliver to help me, and I would always have Matthew's hand to hold. My seventh surgery was scheduled for February, 2009.

The lensectomy in my left eye went well. I had a few weeks of pressure problems, and I ended up with intense "floaters" in the left eye but that was it. Once my eye healed, the vision in both eyes was nearly equal. I couldn't see my hand in front of my face but they were equal! My body was still fighting to relax and release the stress, especially since I had virtually no vision in either eye. I was working very hard just to function throughout the day; it was exhausting trying to get around without hurting myself. A few months had passed and my doctor decided it was time to try to fit me for contacts. Glasses were attempted, but my eyes would not work together and I couldn't tolerate them because of the strength of my prescription. My nearsighted vision most of my life was a -18, when they removed my lenses, I became severely farsighted, I was now a +20!

I had an incredible doctor who specialized in contact lens fittings at the University. He worked tirelessly with me. After about six attempts to have my unique contacts designed, we had success. I was given a new pair of contact lenses for both eyes in June, 2009.

The contacts were hard, gas permeable lenses. They were extremely strong, the world seemed magnified, almost sickeningly clear, but I adjusted quickly. Because they were so strong and thick, they weren't very comfortable, I could feel them in my eye constantly, but being able to see out of both of my eyes again was incredible. My best corrected vision would fluctuate between 20/60 and 20/80.

I was severely farsighted and without lenses, I was unable to focus on anything for very long. It was nearly impossible to read and write. I was only able to read a couple of paragraphs using a magnifying glass. Because of the way my contacts corrected my vision, I viewed the world with my eyes looking somewhat up and out. Trying to read, write or focus on any one thing or person required my eyes to work extremely hard; I needed to pull my eyes inward to focus. It was exhausting just trying to make it through the day. As challenging as it was, I was so very thankful to be able to use both of my eyes again. In early 2010, we were able to celebrate one year without an eye surgery.

Even though I didn't have perfect corrected vision, I was experiencing things I wasn't able to before. I felt like that little six year old girl who was seeing things for the first time. I was overjoyed at seeing so many things again. I could see down the street. When we would take a drive, I could see a little bit of the horizon beyond, I had never been able to do that. I felt so blessed that my doctors were able to come up with a way for me to see the world again, it didn't matter that is wasn't perfect, my eyes were healthy again. I was on a regular, monthly checkup schedule with my eye surgeon.

There were a few problems that occurred but it seemed as though the worst was over.

I continued to take the bus with Oliver everywhere I went, unless Matthew drove me. I didn't feel I could handle the task of driving at that time. Driving requires an enormous amount of focusing and eye energy use. I knew I wasn't ready and that was ok. I had learned to rely on and enjoy public transportation. I also had learned to ask others for help, which was a difficult thing to do. It was very humbling and I was grateful for the wonderful friends who gave their time and went out of their way to help me.

As time passed without more eye trauma events, Matthew and I started talking about moving out of Washington. We had grown so tired of the gloomy, wet weather and yearned for a new start. We weren't sure where we would move to, one thing we were sure of was we would only go where the sun shined, a lot! We attempted to leave Washington a few times through transfers with Matthew's work, but they didn't work out for one reason or another. We knew we would leave someday. We realized that if we were patient, the perfect opportunity would present itself.

My contacts were doing their job well. I had many uncomfortable days, but I was able to adapt. As I became more confident with my new vision, Matthew and I felt it would be ok for me to try driving again. One afternoon, I asked Matthew for the keys to the car. I told him I just wanted to drive through the neighborhood. I got behind the wheel, rolled the windows down and turned on the radio. I drove through our neighborhood for about twenty minutes with a huge smile on my face! It didn't matter that I had no destination and that I was just driving around the block, the sheer joy of driving, that feeling of true freedom was amazing. Driving is not a right; it truly is a privilege that I knew I would never take for granted again.

Since we only had one car, I wasn't able to drive very often which was fine. It was very draining on me visually and I so enjoyed riding the bus with my Oliver. When I did drive, man it was intoxicating!

My parents still lived in Arizona. They were getting up in age and were experiencing health issues. One of the things I worried most about when I was going through my eye surgeries was how I would help my parents when the time came that they needed me. How could I help them when I could barely see and couldn't drive? It was sad for me to think that I might need more help than they would. But the incredible gift of my new contact lenses and the ability to drive again, even though it was limited, gave me such peace of mind. I still had many limitations and had to be very careful, but if they ever needed me, I felt confident I could be there for them.

I could have never predicted that one year later, they would need me more than any of us could have ever imagined.

Chapter 17

GOODBYE

On August 26th of 2010, I was going to turn 50. On December 31st we would celebrate our twentieth wedding anniversary. We had been through so much and had so much to be thankful for, we decided to have a big celebration at our home. We wanted to share with our family and friends the joy we felt from winning a long hard fought battle, and we wanted to, once again share our love with everyone who had been so good to us. The party was planned for August 21st. It would be a combination birthday party for me and Matthew and I were going to renew our wedding vows. We had so much fun planning that event. We invited many friends and family members. Our final rsvp total was seventy. Matthew had built a beautiful arch that stood at the end of our large backyard. We were going to stand under it to renew our vows. We had food and drinks planned, my brother, both my sisters and my niece were going to fly in to celebrate with us. The color scheme for our event included the color purple, so we had a purple bow tie to put around Oliver's neck! He looked so cute wearing it.

Everything was set to go, but two weeks before our party I received a call from my Dad that my Mom had broken her hip and was in the hospital. I could hear the fear and anxiety in his voice, he needed help and support. Dad had just turned eighty at the end of July. He had slowed down quite a bit and hadn't been feeling well himself. My brother and sisters all worked full time so we decided it would be best if I flew to Phoenix to see how I could help. I was afraid of what I would find when I got there, but so happy that I was healed well enough to help them, the one thing I thought I would never be able to do again. It was such an incredible feeling. I felt strong, independent and capable.

Prior to Mom breaking her hip, Mom and Dad had sold their house. They had come to realize with their health issues, they should be closer to family. They were planning to move to Salt Lake City to be near my brother and sister and their families. They had found a beautiful place to live; we were very excited and relieved that they had finally made that decision. My Mom's hip surgery went well and was healing well; however, emotionally she was not doing well. She decided she didn't want to move to Salt Lake after all. She didn't want to leave her home of thirty years. Mom and Dad had some tough conversations about it but in his effort to make Mom happy, Dad told his realtor to cancel the sale of the house.

When I arrived in Phoenix, Dad was physically and emotionally spent. He was worried about Mom; he was not getting good oxygen to his legs and could barely walk ten feet without feeling like he would collapse. I tried to convince him to go to the doctor, but he refused. There was no convincing him, he was stubborn. Dad and I talked one evening about the house. I helped him understand that it was more important than ever that he and Mom move to Salt Lake City. I helped him to see that they needed to have a support system around them, considering Mom's recent injury and the uncertainty of his health. He agreed, we called his realtor and got the house back on the market right away. It had only been a few days, but the previous buyer had already moved on. Dad was so mad at himself, he said he just got scared and didn't want Mom to be upset. It was hard to see him so unsure of himself and the decisions he was making. I could tell the weight of the world came off his shoulders when we got the house on the market again.

I stayed in Phoenix for about six days. We visited Mom every day. Considering the circumstances, Dad and I had a wonderful visit. We spent a lot of time together that week and I felt we became closer than we had ever been. He did accept his inability to walk very far and let me push him in a wheelchair in the hospital when we went to visit Mom. He was a funny guy and would joke around with people and say "If I had known how easy and fun a wheelchair was, I would have had one years ago!" We had great laughs racing through the hospital. I would pretend I was out of control and was going to run into things or crash. My Dad and I had always laughed a lot together, and that week was no exception.

We secured a spot for Mom at a physical rehab center. We both felt good about it and I was comforted knowing she would be safe there for several weeks and Dad didn't have to walk very far to get in and out of there. While I was still in town, we explained to Mom the house was for sale again and why it was so important to get them to Salt Lake. She was very angry with both of us, but we knew it was the right thing to do. She could rehabilitate her hip and Dad could get the house sold again. The plan seemed perfect. Dad and I decided it was a good time for me to go home. The situation still felt very fragile and it was so hard for me to leave, but he told me it was best for me to go home. He said he may need me again down the road so I should get home to Matthew, have our celebration party and wait for the good news that the house was sold, Mom was better and they were on their way to Salt Lake.

I said my painful goodbyes to both of them. Dad took both of my hands in his and kissed them. He told me he loved me and thanked me for the help I had been to them. We were both crying. We were sad, scared, exhausted, relieved and excited all at the same time. I told him how much I loved him and reassured him everything would be fine. My drive to the airport was a long one, mainly because I stopped and turned the car around twice thinking I shouldn't leave. I was so torn inside. I called Dad and asked him again if I should go home, he assured me that it was the best thing for me to do. Then he got grumpy with me and said to stop worrying so much. So, I went home.

It was so good to get home to Matthew and Oliver; I had missed them so much. Matthew and I talked on the phone every day that I was in Phoenix, but we still missed each other a lot. I missed my sweet Oliver, too. The final details of the party were complete. Because of what was happening with Mom and Dad, a bit of the excitement for the party had been dampened but we were still looking forward to it. We had each written the renewal vows we would say to each other, it was going to be a beautiful night. I was so excited to see my family. It was the first time in 15 years that the four of us (my siblings) would be together at the same time. It was going to be such a special time for us.

Four days after I got home, Mom was taken to the rehab center. She was unhappy there the minute she arrived. She stayed one night and the next morning when my Dad visited her, she told him she was not going to stay there. They had quite an argument about it, the doctors and nurses tried to explain to my Mom that she needed the rehab so her hip would heal properly and she could get stronger. There was no convincing her. The medical staff reluctantly signed the forms to release her. Dad had a medical transport van take her home. She was completely immobile. They took her home, put her in her bed and left. Dad called and told me and reassured me that he could take care of her just fine. Matthew and I knew that it wouldn't end well.

All of us kids held our breath, and called them a few times a day to check on them. We could hear the tension in Dad's voice and tried to get a true sense of how things were going. We didn't have to wait long, three days after Mom came home, their good friend and neighbor called; she was at their home with Dad. They both believed he was having a heart attack and needed to go to the hospital. He refused to call 911 so their neighbor drove him to the hospital. I called their other neighbor and she went over to be with Mom until I could get there later that night. Needless to say, the party was off. I was on a plane back to Phoenix three hours later.

When I arrived in Phoenix, I had just enough light outside left to get my rental car and drive to Mom and Dad's house. I got a crash course from their neighbor how to take care of Mom who was still immobile and using a bed pan. Their poor neighbor had been there for twelve hours; I sent her home and sat with Mom for a while. I was able to get her to eat some dinner and take her medicine before she drifted off to sleep. I called the neighbor who took Dad to the hospital and she came over to take me to the hospital to see him.

I walked into Dad's hospital room and the poor man looked awful. He had tubes coming out of him everywhere. He had suffered a minor heart attack and was having trouble breathing. He was in a horrible mood. He was angry at everyone and everything and he was worried about Mom. I tried to reassure him everything would be alright and that he needed to rest and take care of himself. By the time I got home that night I was completely exhausted. I wasn't used to such a full day of using my eyes, I needed desperately to sleep and rest my eyes.

That night was very hard. Mom needed my help and would call out to me every hour, she was in her bedroom downstairs and I was upstairs. My eyes could not handle my contacts anymore so I had to care for her blind. I went down the stairs on my hands and knees because I couldn't walk down them safely. After doing that a couple of times I just laid in the recliner outside her room so that I could be near her. I slept for about two hours that night. The next morning I took care of Mom's needs and then her neighbor came over again to look after her while I went to the hospital to see Dad.

I was beyond exhausted and I was experiencing a lot of pain in my eyes. I knew I couldn't do it alone. I called my sister and asked her to please come to Phoenix to help. She was able to get a flight to Phoenix that evening. Her best friend in Phoenix picked her up from the airport and brought her to Mom and Dad's home. I was so happy to see her, we hugged each other so tight, both of us feeling very uncertain and frightened at the thought of what would happen next.

When I got to the hospital the next morning there were several doctors in the room with my Dad. I sat in a quiet room waiting for them to come talk with me. The first doctor came and told me Dad had pneumonia and severe emphysema. More tests were being done and I was told the results would be back the next morning. The tests revealed that all of the arteries going into his heart were ninety percent blocked. After I was given that devastating news I called my brother and other sister and told them it wasn't looking very good for Dad and they should probably come to Arizona right away. When I returned to the hospital later that afternoon, another doctor had been running tests on my Dad, she was a lung specialist. She was a wonderful, kind doctor with a big heart. She had really grown to like my Dad and I could tell it was hard for her to tell me the latest diagnosis. She proceeded to tell me that in addition to everything else, Dad had a large tumor on his lung. He had terminal lung cancer that was inoperable.

They explained everything to my Dad, he understood how sick he was and he accepted the news with ease as if he was already keenly aware of how sick he was. He told my sister he was so happy with the life he had lived, he had no regrets. We didn't know how long Dad would live but it was suggested we get him transferred to hospice.

My sisters were at my parents' home still attending to Mom's needs and trying to get the house in order because the sale was scheduled to close within six days. My brother was back and forth between the hospital and banks trying to get financial affairs in order for my parents. In the meantime, Matthew loaded up the car and Oliver and drove to Salt Lake City. He and my sister-in-law were there trying to find a hospice location for my Dad. I was making arrangements to get my Dad transported to Salt Lake City, driving all over Phoenix gathering medical records for my Mom and exploring options of how we were going to get her to Salt Lake City, too. There were six of us working on that situation. We would get one problem solved and another one would take its place. It was stressful and exhausting, and while we all had to keep our focus on our jobs, the sad reality was that Dad was going to die, soon. We had to tell Mom, our hearts were breaking. Mom and Dad had only been able to speak on the phone one time while he was in the hospital; they told each other they loved one another for the very last time.

I arranged to have my Dad flown to Salt Lake City on a medical flight the next day from a small regional airport. My brother flew with him and my sisters, niece and I stood at the edge of the runway and watched as the jet carrying my Dad disappeared into the sky. It was so emotional, so sad, and we all cried, but it was also one of the most beautiful moments in our lives, a moment in our lives that could never be forgotten. After Dad was settled into hospice, he was fading quickly. I spoke to him very briefly on the phone. I said. "You are the best Dad in the world; I love you very much, goodbye."

I arranged for my Mom to be flown to Salt Lake City on a medical flight a few days later, on my fiftieth birthday. She was going into a rehab center there to recover while her hip healed. On the morning of my birthday, we were waiting for the medical transport to pick up my Mom and take her to the airport. My brother called just before they arrived to tell us Dad had passed away earlier that morning. It was hard to explain, but at that moment, I felt a bond stronger than I ever had to my Dad. He went to heaven on the fiftieth anniversary of my birth; it was painful and beautiful at the same time.

We said our sad goodbyes to my sister and my niece and watched them drive away as they headed home to California. My other sister and I flew with my Mom to Salt Lake City. The scenery from that small plane was beautiful; we saw a view of the Grand Canyon that was incredible. The medical team suggested we wait until after the flight to tell Mom about Dad's passing. Keeping it from her was extremely difficult but we knew it was the right thing to do for her.

After we got her settled into her room at the rehab center, I stood next to my brother as he told Mom the love of her life was gone. That poor woman had lost everything overnight, her health, her home and now her husband; our hearts were poured out for her.

My Mom was so sweet; she insisted we have a little party for my birthday in her room that night. The whole family had cake and champagne, as I opened a few gifts. It was a beautiful, but heartbreaking night. There was a lot of love in that room.

Chapter 18

A WARM BLANKET

The drive back to Washington from Utah was long and oh so sad. I shed a lot of tears at the thought of never seeing my Dad again, but I also smiled as I thought of so many wonderful memories of him. I was filled with peace knowing my Mom was safe, getting the medical attention she needed, and that she was surrounded by family that loved her dearly. I didn't know what was ahead of us, but I was certain that we would all be just fine.

Even though it was late August, we were welcomed back to Washington by the usual gray skies and soggy ground. It was really good to get home, though. It felt so good to sleep in our own bed and to begin getting life back to normal. We had a wonderful Thanksgiving with our good friends, a peaceful, relaxing Christmas and a much deserved twentieth anniversary that we shared with a small group of very special friends; it was a beautiful New Year's celebration.

As January was passing, Matthew and I realized how lucky we were, but deep down, there was still that desire, that need to get out of Washington. It broke our hearts to think of leaving the great friends we'd made and we loved the house, but it was time, we needed the sun and we were determined to find a way to get to it.

We had conversations about how we could leave but there just didn't seem to be a way out, until one day Matthew came home and said to me, "Linda, I think I have figured out a way we can leave Washington and get back to the warmth of the Arizona sunshine." He said, "How does going back to Phoenix sound to you?" I couldn't believe what he was saying; I was thinking *how in the world could we go back to Phoenix?* I knew the position he held wasn't available in Phoenix. He had crunched some numbers and figured out that because of the lower cost of living in Arizona, especially the cost of homes, he would take a demotion and we could make it financially. He had only five years left until he could retire from the agency he worked for. He was willing to take the risk that he wouldn't get his current position back, his paycheck would be smaller, and his hours wouldn't be as good. It's amazing how desperate you become and what you are willing to give up when you really want out of your current situation!

After a few days of sleeping on it and having many long conversations about it, we agreed, we were going back to Phoenix! We never thought we'd move back there, but we knew, without a doubt, it was what we wanted. It would be bittersweet to return because of the absence of my parents and Matthew's sister and her husband had moved out of Arizona, but the thought of getting back to the place and life we knew we loved and had missed was so exciting! Within two weeks, Matthew had put in for a transfer and we put our house up for sale. We didn't know how long it would take for his transfer to come through or how long it would take to sell the house, but we were ready to start the ball rolling and had faith it would all work out.

Three weeks later our house was sold! We moved into an apartment not knowing how long we would be in it, but with the house sold, we could leave at a moment's notice if we needed to. Oliver was so good, he adjusted to apartment living very quickly, got used to not having his back yard and having to be on a leash most of the time outside. He was so adaptable, we weren't surprised.

Three months later, Matthew was offered a position in Phoenix. We had one month to find somewhere to live, get packed and hit the road. We started our search for a new home in Arizona. As we and our realtor searched for what we wanted, we discovered an absolutely gorgeous new community on the computer. The housing market in Arizona was trying to recover, so we didn't expect to find a brand new home but we got incredibly lucky and found the perfect home in the perfect location. Matthew flew to Phoenix on a Friday, looked at a model of our home, and walked through the newly framed house that we would buy on Saturday. One of our friends in Phoenix asked him how it felt to walk out of the airport into 110 degree heat in July. He said, "It felt like a nice warm blanket." The exact house and lot we wanted, in the city, and even better, at a price that will probably never be seen again in our lifetime! It was so wonderful; the new future in front of us looked as though things were going our way, finally!!

We closed on our new home on my birthday in 2012, one year to the day of my Dad's death. I believed in my heart that Dad had orchestrated the whole thing from heaven. Thanks Dad!

Oliver and I flew to Phoenix and stayed in a hotel for a few days while Matthew drove all of our belongings to Arizona. Even though he was alone, he was excited about the future; he said that was one of the most enjoyable road trips he had ever taken. When Oliver and I stepped outside at the Phoenix airport, I looked up, saw that blue sky and that big, beautiful sun and felt the healing rays immediately.

Oliver and I were the first to see our brand new home, it was so beautiful! I called Matthew as he was driving to tell him that Oliver and I were standing on the front sidewalk looking at the house. I was so excited, describing to him how the outside looked. I stood frozen in disbelief that it was our home. As I spoke with Matthew on the phone, Oliver and I made our way up our beautiful entry, unlocked the front door and walked in. We stood in the entry for a few seconds, looked around, looked at each other and went from room to room. I smiled as Oliver's tail was wagging so fast while he trotted around, I was giggling and describing every detail to Matthew, we were so giddy!

It was difficult ending that conversation, and letting go of all of the exhilaration, but Matthew needed to focus on driving so we said our goodbyes, anxious to be together in a few days. Oliver and I stayed in the house, lay on the beautiful new carpet, and had a little picnic in the middle of our empty living room. That was another very special moment that I got to share with Oliver, I felt so happy and blessed.

Matthew arrived a few days later and we moved in to our house. Construction on our new swimming pool began a few weeks after we moved in. We got such a good price on the home we didn't have to wait for the pool, which we considered to be a necessity, not a luxury in the Arizona heat. The pool was completed in four weeks and the landscaping of the backyard was completed shortly after. The pool was gorgeous, framed at the far end by a rock waterfall. Even though it was Fall when the pool was completed and it was too cool to swim, we enjoyed sitting around it, day and night. The temperatures outside were perfect during the day, and at night we sat out with a light jacket on, turned on the waterfall, lit our tiki torches and looked at the stars. Matthew and I would look at each other and just smile, from knowing that moving back to Arizona was one of the best decisions we had ever made.

Oliver loved Arizona, too. He would lie outside in the grass and sun himself for a while, come inside and cool off on the tile floor, take a long nap, go outside and do it all over again. It was obvious to us that he loved his new home as much as we did.

The hours Matthew worked were tough, and the work wasn't what he really wanted to do again, but he never minded going in to work. He didn't care what he had to do so long as he could be, as he put it, "Draped in the warm blanket of the Arizona sun." Matthew's hard work and sacrifice paid off. About six months after we moved back, an individual retired and the same position he had worked at in Washington came available in Arizona. He applied for the job, and he got it. He was promoted back to the position that he sacrificed so that we could relocate and it was the position that he enjoyed. He was back to working Monday through Friday, with weekends and holidays off. Good things come to good people, and if anyone deserved good fortune it was Matthew.

I am finishing my story in the early Fall of 2013. Every day, our new life in Arizona is just what we hoped for.

Matthew enjoys his work, in the summer he walks in the door, gets out of his work clothes and jumps in the pool and his day just melts away. He's looking forward to retiring in a few years and starting a new career. He gets to see the sun over three hundred days a year and, as always comes home every day to a wife and poodle that love and adore him.

Oliver is loving life, too. He has made some new dog friends that he sees from time to time, he usually gets two walks every day to the park and he runs, sniffs and plays. He's had some challenging health issues this past year, he had an intestinal infection that prevented him from eating to the point it appeared we would lose him. He ended up in intensive care for two days because he wasn't able to eat anything for six days. We have a great veterinarian that took very good care of him. Oliver has bounced back and is doing better. He still has struggles with his appetite, but his medications are helping him. There are times when we have to coax him to eat by playing games or by hand feeding him, which can be time consuming and inconvenient, but he's worth every second of it. I actually consider it a privilege, not a chore because he's been so loyal and helpful to me. I would hand feed him for the rest of his life, if that's what he needs.

I am doing quite well. Although it could change at any time, right now my eye health has remained stable, but I have days that are more difficult than others. Without my natural lenses, it's difficult for me to focus. I'm still not able to read or write. I plan my daily activities wisely to prevent overworking my eyes or I suffer the consequences with extreme fatigue and pain. If I overdo it, I'm unable to wear my contacts and have no vision left by the evening. I can be on the computer for short periods of time with my screen enlarged to two hundred percent. I usually get on the computer at night right before bed. If I use it more than just a few minutes during the day, I suffer.

When I wear my contacts, my vision fluctuates between 20/60 and 20/70. I had always wondered what my vision was without my contacts. I could never get a clear answer from my doctors. Finally my new contact lens doctor did a very simple test and told Matthew and I the number. We didn't think there was anything left that an eye doctor could say that would shock us, but we were wrong. She told us my vision, without correction, was 20/14,000. Matthew and I were speechless, and I know both our hearts skipped a beat.

I have every room in my house and my front and back yards memorized, but without my contacts, I need to be very careful. Needless to say, I take very good care of my contacts.

I'm not able to have any hobbies because everything requires so much focusing. I do enjoy listening to audio books, and I still dance and exercise. I always imagined my life would be much different than it is at my age, but I'm not complaining, I'm very happy. I am so lucky that I didn't lose my eyesight completely, it could be so much worse. I spend my days taking care of Matthew, Oliver and our home, how could I feel bad about any of that? Because I am able to drive short distances during the day, I got a new car. I drive a fun, little Honda Fit. I run my errands and visit with friends. For about a year, I was volunteering with Oliver as a pet therapy team at a physical rehab center near our home. The patients loved him; we both got a lot of joy out of that experience. So many people had helped me; it felt so good to give back. Because of Oliver's health issues and his age, I had to make the difficult decision to retire him from pet therapy as well as being my service dog. Of course, I feel more confident and miss having him with me when I go out into the world but he is getting old and it is too hard on him. He gets to spend his days relaxing, which he deserves. Every so often I will take him out with me somewhere, and he still wags his tail with excitement when I put his service vest on him.

It took nearly two years for my doctor to improve and duplicate my contacts, but we finally got there. I currently have a pair that is bearable, I struggle daily with my vision but I have adjusted, accepted my limitations, and am at peace with it.

As visually challenging as it's been for me to write my story it's been an amazing part of my journey. My Arizona eye doctor encouraged me to tell my story to help heal the emotional wounds that I've suffered as a result of so many traumatic events over such a long period of time. She is amazing and she was right. She gave me perfect advice because telling my story has lifted much of the heaviness, and has turned my focus from the trauma to a sense of awe for having gone through all that I have and ending up being so blessed by where I am today.

My strongest desire is that my story will lift others who are facing challenges great and small and bring hope into their lives. No matter what struggles we endure in life, we can come out on the other side, even happier and better than we were before. It's not in my DNA to give up and stop believing that I can get through anything. I am strong and will always choose to see that my glass is half full.

My wish is that anyone who reads this story will also recognize their own strength, and never stop believing in a brighter day.

Prologue

In the Fall of 2013, I worked on some finishing touches to the book, and started to learn how to self-publish. It was finally finished, or so I thought…..

A few days before Thanksgiving, I received a call from my brother and sister, telling me that Mom had taken a bad fall and was not doing well. Matthew, Oliver and I left Arizona on Thanksgiving Day to be with her. I prayed we would get to her in time. We did make it to her, but sadly, she passed away on December 4, 2013. It was very hard to say goodbye to her, but I knew she was at peace and not suffering anymore. I had the chance to thank her for being a wonderful Mother and tell her how much I loved her. Mom didn't get to finish reading my book. I had been giving her chapters to read as I completed them, she was able to finish 10 chapters. I wish both my Mom and Dad could be here to see the finished product, but what matters most was that they knew I was happy and doing well.

Although I was grieving the loss of my Mom, I knew I needed to keep working to get my book published. After a couple of months I got back to work on it. But as luck would have it, another big bump in the road came along. I went for my annual retina check-up and my doctor discovered severe swelling on the retina in my right eye. Things had been so quiet since 2010. I thought the worst was over. That day I received an injection of medicine into my eye. I would see her again in a month to determine what was next. The following month, we all decided the best course of action would be to implant a tiny, self-dissolving medication rod into my eye that would slowly release medication to my retina over a three month period.

Right before my implant, we discovered a growth on Oliver's right eye, it was scratching his cornea. He also had several benign tumors on his body that needed to be removed. We decided to get Oliver's surgery done right after the implant was done. We felt comfortable with this decision because the implant would be working quietly inside my eye, helping it heal. Oliver was pretty banged up after having so many things removed from his body and his eye. He needed constant monitoring. He needed eye drops, antibiotics and pain medications twice a day.

Oliver and I were both home recovering, and then, six days after the implant was put in my eye, it "torpedoed" through my pupil and slammed into my cornea. I had to have emergency surgery to remove the implant. My doctors were in complete shock, as this had never happened before. Story of my life! Luckily my cornea healed quickly and I was able to wear my contact again. A few weeks after the implant surgery, I had to have another injection to address the swelling that was still present on the retina. Six days after that injection, my retina detached. I had to have another emergency surgery to repair it. They discovered that two membranes had formed on the retina and one of them tore it. The surgeon had to repair the tear and do two membrane peels. After the retina surgery I had to lay face down for one week because a gas bubble was put in my eye to seal and protect the surgery area. In a period of ten weeks, I had two injections, an implant that failed, and two surgeries!

The recovery from so many traumas in such a short period of time was extremely difficult; but slowly I began to get back to normal. The vision in the right eye is still not very good but I am managing. It took about three weeks for Oliver to completely heal, but he is doing very well. It was grueling for Matthew and I trying to take care of Oliver and me, too.

A very good friend asked me how I was managing to get through it all. I thought about it for a few minutes and I realized that I reverted back to that place of strength that I draw from. I made a conscious effort to take it a day at a time and focus on the good in my life. I also still have an incredible support system. Matthew, Oliver, my family and friends helped me immensely.

Life can be very hard. Sometimes the struggles we face feel like they will be impossible to overcome. I am certain I will have more challenges with my eyes as time goes by, but I will face them head on. There is a phrase in a song I love that says "With every broken bone, I swear I lived!" That's what I'm doing, making the most of every day and loving every second of it!

The End...or maybe, just the beginning.

Matthew, Linda and Oliver, 2014

We love our back yard!

Mom and Linda, 1966

Soon after the first time I saw her face.

Linda, 1968

Decided to have my school picture without my glasses

Linda, 1969

Prettiest glasses ever!

My wonderful family, 1966

Linda and Oliver, 2014

Recovering together

Linda and Matthew, 2014

We found some shade to stand in!

Oliver, 2012

Professional portrait session.
The photographer said he posed
better than most people.

So handsome in his service
vest!

Oliver, 2013

"I think I see a rabbit!"

Oliver, 2014

**Just relaxing in the back yard, he
loves Arizona.**

45101231R00072

Made in the USA
Columbia, SC
20 December 2018